Would you like to learn to be a better baker?

We know that so many people watch *The Great British Bake Off* for the tips and techniques you pick up – not only from the judges, but from watching the bakers too. We wanted to distil that knowledge into a library of cookbooks that are specifically designed to take you from novice to expert baker. Individually, each book covers the skills you will want to perfect so that you can master a particular area of baking – everything from cakes to bread, sweet pastries to pies.

We have chosen recipes that are classics of each type, and grouped them together so that they take you on a progression from 'Easy does it' through 'Needs a little skill' to 'Up for a challenge'. Put together, the full series of books will give you a comprehensive collection of the best recipes, along with all the advice you need to become a better baker.

The triumphs and lessons of the bakers in the tent show us that not everything works every time. But I hope that with these books as your guide, we have given you a head start towards baking it better every time!

Linda Collister
Series Editor

- BAKE IT BETTER -
BREAD

Linda Collister

HODDER &
STOUGHTON

Contents

BAKE IT BETTER
Baker's Guide

BAKE IT BETTER
Recipes

Easy does it   30

Needs a little skill 112

Up for a challenge 154

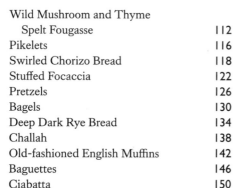

Welcome bakers!

There is great joy to be found in cutting a thick slice of home-made bread, and this book gives you 40 classic bread recipes to start you off.

As well as being great bakes, these recipes have been selected to introduce you to all the key skills like mixing, kneading, proving and shaping that not only give you better bread, but which you will find useful in many other future bakes.

Start with the 'Easy does it' section and get the basics under your belt with recipes like Farmhouse White Soda Bread or tasty Cornbread. As you get a little more sure of your baking, move on to the recipes that 'Need a little skill' – colourful Stuffed Focaccia perhaps, soft, golden Pretzels, or some Old-Fashioned English Muffins, dripping with butter and jam. As you bake more, you will soon be 'Up for a challenge', using all your new breadmaking skills to produce the stunning Harvest Wreath, or spectacular Nine-Strand Plaited Loaf.

The colour strip on the right-hand side of the page tells you at a glance the level of difficulty of the recipe (from one spoon for easy to three spoons for more of a challenge), and gives you a helpful checklist of the skills and special equipment you will use. Before you begin, have a look at the Baker's Guide at the beginning of the book. This will tell you what equipment you need to get started (just a bowl, a spoon and a loaf tin will do!), introduce you to the most important ingredients, and explain some terms and techniques in more detail.

Bread can be a simple piece of toast, or the heart of a whole meal, but every loaf can be impressive. With *Bake It Better: Bread* to show you just what you can do with flour, salt, yeast and water, it's time to get out your mixing bowl and start baking.

HOW TO USE THE BAKE IT BETTER BOOKS

SECTION 1: BAKER'S GUIDE
Read this section before you start baking. The Baker's Guide contains key information on ingredients (page 10–13), equipment (pages 14–17) and skills (pages 18–25) relevant to the recipes in the book.

Refer back the Baker's Guide when you're baking if you want a refresher on a particular skill. In the recipes the first mention of each skill is highlighted in bold.

SECTION 2: THE RECIPES
Colour strips on the right-hand side and 1, 2 or 3 spoons show the level of difficulty of the recipe. Within the colour strips you'll find helpful information to help you decide what to bake: Hands-on time; Hands-off time; Baking time; Makes/Serves; Special equipment; Storage.

Refresh your knowledge of any Essential skills by referring to the Baker's Guide before you get started.

Refer back to the Baker's Guide when a skill is highlighted in bold in the recipe if you need a reminder.

Try Something Different options are given where the recipe lends itself to experimenting with ingredients or decorations.

BAKE IT BETTER

Baker's Guide

Ingredients

The great thing about bread is that just four main ingredients will give you a delicious loaf: flour, salt, yeast and water. But change these ingredients – for example add a different flour, or substitute buttermilk for water – and your bread will be transformed. Here are a few guidelines to keep in mind when buying, storing and using your ingredients.

CORNMEAL

Yellow and white cornmeals are made from the whole kernels of corn or maize which are ground to a fine, medium or coarse texture. The meal is very low in gluten and is usually mixed with wheat flour for yeasted bread, but you can also sprinkle it under and on top of soft doughs to prevent sticking and to create a crisp, crunchy crust.

FLOUR

Flour is probably the most important ingredient in baking, but especially so in bread-making; poor-quality or past-its-best flour can really affect the final taste and texture of your loaf. As with all ingredients, flour should be used when fresh, so store it correctly – to stop it getting damp keep opened packs in storage jars, plastic food boxes or in plastic food bags. Don't add new flour to old in storage jars and use it within a month of opening, or by its best before date. Keep an eye on wholemeal flours and flours with added grains as they spoil quicker than refined flours, and don't use flour that smells slightly rancid or contains weevils or mites.

Flour is usually ground from wheat, but there is a good range of flours made from other grains.

Wheat flours are probably the most commonly used flours in baking.

Stoneground flour is produced when cereal grains (wheat, rye, oats, etc.) are milled between two large stones, instead of the steel rollers used for mass-produced flours, and has a different texture and often a fuller flavour. **Plain** and **self-raising flours** have 8–10 per cent protein (ideal for non-yeast breads, as well as cakes and pastries); **strong bread flour** has 12–16 per cent protein (ideal for most breads); and **extra-strong** or **extra-strong Canadian flour** has 15–17 per cent protein (ideal for bagels or for making larger loaves).

Wheat flours are our staple and, like all flours, are defined by their rate of extraction – how much of the entire wheat grain or kernel is used in the flour. **White flour** usually contains about 75 per cent of the kernel and has most of the bran and wheatgerm removed. **Brown flour** usually contains around 85 per cent of the kernel (the extraction rate is stated on the pack as there's no standard amount) and contains most of the wheatgerm, but has some of the bran removed. **Wholemeal or wholegrain flour** has 100 per cent extraction, which means the complete kernel is ground. The high proportion of bran in the flour – those coarse golden specks – means your loaf won't rise as well as one made with all-white flour, as the bran hinders gluten development, but the flavour and health benefits will be greater. Some wheat flours have malted wheat grains added to give a sweeter taste and slightly crunchy texture.

Wheat flour for bread-making is labelled as 'bread flour' or 'strong flour', as it contains flour milled from wheat with a higher proportion of protein to starch than that used for pastry and cakes. It's the protein content that's key to yeasted bread-making: as the dough is kneaded, the protein develops into strands of gluten, which help the dough to rise by expanding around the gases produced by the yeast. **Speciality wheat flours** are available for ciabatta (with around 10 per cent protein), pizza (with some durum wheat and 12–16 per cent protein), and baguettes (around 12 per cent protein – look out for the French Type 55) as these flours are made from wheat varieties specifically grown to make these breads.

Barley flour is low in gluten so the loaves tend to be dense, but a little added to a dough made with wheat or rye flour adds flavour.

Oat flour is not as widely available as oatmeal, oatflakes or porridge oats, but can be quickly made in a food-processor from oatflakes, and when mixed with wheat flour makes a textured, tasty loaf.

Rye flour was once a staple in places where the soil was too poor, or too cold, for wheat, but is now popular for its deep flavour and dark, chewy crumb; it works best in a sourdough mixture. Rye flour has a low gluten content, which makes it harder to work than wheat flours, but some find it easier to digest. Look out for wholegrain rye, which is darker than the finer 'light' rye, which has some of the bran sifted out.

Spelt flour has been grown throughout Europe for centuries. It comes from the same family as common wheat, but is more nutritious and higher in protein. Spelt flour is available as both wholegrain and 'white', and makes a really good, well-flavoured loaf.

Gluten-free flours are wheat-free mixtures of several flours made from rice, potato, chickpea, tapioca, sorghum, broad bean, maize and buckwheat, depending on the brand. (Try different brands, as they vary in flavour.) Some flour mixes also contain xanthum gum, which replaces gluten in giving structure to the dough. Check the label; if your mix doesn't include it, see the recipe on page 86 or add 1 tsp xanthum gum per 150g flour. Gluten-free flours need more liquid than wheat-flour doughs, so you can't replace them exactly with the wheat flour.

Cut grains and flakes can be added to dough, along with the flour, for extra texture, or sprinkled on top before baking. **Cut wheat, spelt or rye** is the whole grain cut into two or three pieces; **wheat or spelt flakes** are made by steaming, then rolling, the kernel. You can add **cut rye** to add flavour and texture to pumpernickel and rye breads.

LIQUIDS

There's no need to use bottled or spring water: tap water is fine. Some bakers prefer to use filtered water that's been boiled, and cooled, to remove any chlorine – this is most relevant for sourdoughs because chlorine can hinder growth of the cultures.

Many recipes replace some, or all, of the water with other ingredients. Make sure you add all the liquids at the temperature stated in the recipe. If they are too warm they will kill the yeast. **Milk** gives the bread a finer, softer crumb. If you don't have fresh milk, use powdered milk made up to the correct quantity with cooled boiled water. **Buttermilk** is fermented a bit like yoghurt, and not usually made at home as it needs special cultures and some basic equipment.

Yoghurt is often added to naan as it helps fermentation and flavour. **Eggs** add flavour and enrich the dough, but make it slightly heavier, too. They also add colour, like the golden shade of brioche.

NUTS

All sorts of nuts, such as hazelnuts, walnuts, pecans, almonds and pine nuts can be added to your dough with the flour, or kneaded in towards the end. If you lightly toast them first you'll increase their flavour. Adding a little of their matching oil (such as walnut or hazelnut oil) can intensify the 'nuttiness' of a loaf. Nuts are not usually added as a topping as they burn too easily to cope with the high oven temperature needed for yeasted doughs. Because of their high oil content, check nuts taste fresh before using.

SALT

The recipes in this book use fine sea salt; if you have the coarser, flaked sort, crush it first so that it combines easily with the flour. Salt is added to bread not only for flavour, but also for its role in the development of the dough structure. Most recipes use between 1 and 2g salt per 100g flour, but make sure when adding your salt to the bowl it's kept out of direct contact with the yeast for as long as possible as salt retards yeast growth.

SEEDS

Seeds such as sunflower, sesame, pumpkin and linseed, among others, can be added to doughs along with the flour to give a crunchy texture and boost flavour. Avoid overloading the dough or the bread will be crumbly. Sprinkled on top of a shaped dough, seeds can improve the finished look of baked bread – but take care to avoid burning them.

YEAST

Yeast is the living organism that makes bread rise. It needs moisture, gentle warmth and flour (or sugar) to stimulate its growth and the production of carbon dioxide, which expands the dough. The recipes here use dried powdered yeast, sold in 7g sachets (and tubs) as fast-action, easy-blend or instant dried yeast. They must be kept in a store cupboard. The powder must be added to the flour and dry ingredients (never to the liquid). Hot water kills yeast, while salt retards its growth.

Fresh yeast, sold at wholefood stores, some bakeries and bakery counters in larger supermarkets, is greyish-brown, with a distinct aroma, and feels like clay. It can be stored, tightly wrapped, in a sealed plastic box in the fridge for a week, but should be used before it turns dark brown or powdery grey. Use 15g fresh yeast instead of a 7g sachet fast-action dried yeast; crumble it into a bowl and cream it to a smooth liquid with about 7 tablespoons of your measured liquid, then work in a little of the measured flour and leave for about 15 minutes. When the mixture froths and bubbles it is ready to use – add it to the flour and dry ingredients with the rest of the lukewarm liquid; if your mixture doesn't look frothy, it's not working. Some dried yeast, sold in tubs as 'regular dried yeast', needs to be mixed with a little measured lukewarm liquid and sugar, and left for 15 minutes to 'froth up' before adding to the flour with the remaining liquid – check the pack for instructions.

Use the quantity of yeast specified in the recipe; use more and the dough will be lively but the loaf may have a strong aftertaste and keep less well; use less and the dough will take longer to rise and prove (see page 20), but have a deeper flavour.

Equipment

You don't need fancy equipment for bread-making, but good-quality essentials will make your life easier and give you more consistent results. Here is our list of the basics, plus a few extra bits of kit you might find useful.

BAKING PAPER
Non-stick baking paper and **parchment paper** are best for lining baking sheets and trays. **Greaseproof paper** has a waxy coating that doesn't stand up so well to the heat of the oven.

BAKING SHEETS
These are fantastic. Buy at least one very heavy-duty sheet that won't buckle or warp in a really hot oven so the base stays truly flat. Also, check you get the right size for your oven! Baking sheets have only one raised edge for gripping which means you'll be able to slide your bread on and off it easily. Baking trays have sides all the way round.

BAKING STONE OR PIZZA STONE
This will give your bread the perfect base – better than a hot baking sheet; you can keep it in the oven so that it heats up thoroughly when your oven is on. Measure your oven before you buy one to ensure you get the right size.

BANNETON
A bread proving basket, or banneton, gives a lovely finish to sourdough (see page 164) because of the pattern of the cane or wicker its made from, but a mixing bowl is just as good for proving.

BOWLS
If you're buying new, a nest of small, medium and large bowls is ideal. For versatility, sturdiness (without being overly heavy) and durability, **heatproof glass** and **stainless steel** are both good choices. They can be used for both cold and hot mixtures (such as when melting chocolate over a pan of simmering water). Be aware, though, that stainless steel is not suitable for the microwave. **Plastic** bowls are cheaper and some have a built-in rubber base to help reduce wobble. (Some bowls even come with a non-slip silicone base for this purpose, although you can stabilise any bowl by placing a damp cloth underneath it.) Plastic bowls are, however, quite lightweight and do feel less sturdy to work with. **Ceramic** bowls are pretty and can go in the dishwasher, but they break quite easily and can be heavy. **Anodised aluminium** bowls are very durable and will last a lifetime, but they can't go in the microwave.

A very large bowl with a snap-on lid is extremely useful for mixing and rising large batches of dough (see pages 18 and 20).

CLINGFILM OR TEA TOWELS
For covering dough and proving loaves (see page 20); make sure you use a clean, dry tea towel each time.

COOLING RACKS
At least one large wire cooling rack with legs is essential to let air circulate underneath cooling bread (see page 24). If you need to you can improvise with a clean wire grill-pan rack.

DOUGH SCRAPER
This is one of the cheapest, but definitely most useful pieces of kit for a bread maker. It should be sturdy but flexible, so that you can scoop or scrape up doughs (and

clean bowls), as well as divide them for shaping.

FREE-STANDING MIXER OR FOOD-PROCESSOR

If you do a lot of baking, a large free-standing mixer or food-processor with an attachment for making dough is a great investment, as it really does save a lot of time and energy. If possible, buy an extra bowl, as it helps when batch-baking, and a snap-on lid is a great help for rising and/or chilling doughs (see page 20).

HEAVY-DUTY OVEN GLOVES OR OVEN CLOTH

These are absolutely vital when baking bread and must always be kept dry. Don't ever use a damp tea towel for loading/unloading the oven, as you can burn yourself quite seriously.

KNIVES

A **small, very sharp knife** is used to slash the tops of loaves before baking, while a **large sharp knife** is vital for chopping nuts and slicing (as is a **knife sharpener**); a **round-bladed knife** is handy for cutting up butter, and for 'rubbing in'. A **long-bladed serrated bread knife** is essential for slicing baked loaves, and **kitchen scissors** are useful for snipping the tops of loaves and rolls instead of slashing.

MEASURING JUGS

Pick a heat-resistant and microwave-safe jug with both metric and imperial measures, starting from 50ml, if you can find it, otherwise 100ml, and going up to 2 litres. A small jug or cup that measures from 1 teaspoon (5ml) up to 4 tablespoons (60ml) is a very useful extra. And remember that you can weigh water as well as measure its volume: 1ml = 1 gram. Some bakers prefer this method as it is the most precise.

MEASURING SPOONS

A set of measuring spoons is essential for measuring small amounts of liquids and dry ingredients such as baking powder, spices, salt and sugar. Day-to-day teaspoons, dessertspoons and tablespoons can vary enormously in size and will give inconsistent results. Measuring spoons range from ⅛ teaspoon to 1½ tablespoons. Go for spoons with narrow ends that will fit into fiddly spice jars. Unless otherwise indicated, all spoon measures in these recipes are level – skim off any excess with a finger or the back of a knife.

OVEN THERMOMETER

An oven thermometer is very handy, as oven thermostats can be notoriously unreliable. With a thermometer you can double-check your oven is the correct temperature and work out where the hot and cool spots are located, and adjust your baking accordingly.

PASTRY BRUSH

Available in a variety of widths and bristles, pick a good-quality brush in a medium width for brushing on glaze or brushing away excess flour. Make sure whatever type you buy is heat resistant and dishwasher-proof.

ROLLING PIN

For making shaped and laminated doughs (layered with butter); choose a long, fairly heavy one about 6–7cm in diameter; ones without handles are generally easier to use. Look after your rolling pin and it should last a lifetime, so never leave a wooden rolling pin soaking in washing-up water and don't put it in the dishwasher.

SCALES

Baking is really a science, so it pays to be accurate if you want perfect results every time. As you'll be dealing with some quite small quantities, **digital** scales are preferable to **spring** or **balance** scales as they are much more precise and can weigh ingredients that are as little as 1 gram. You can see the weight easily at a glance and you can add multiple items to one bowl simply by resetting the balance to zero after adding each ingredient. A helpful tip: always keep a spare battery on standby.

STORAGE CONTAINERS

Keeping your home-baked loaves fresh means a special bread bin, purpose-made, if possible, from wood, metal or ceramics, and with a tight-fitting lid. Otherwise use a good stainless-steel tin with a secure lid. Don't store your loaves in a sealed plastic box as this can encourage the bread to sweat and turn mouldy. Store well away from sources of heat (radiators/sunlight/kitchen light fittings/fridge or cooker areas) as this encourages mould to develop. (See page 25 for more on storing your bread.)

TIMER

A digital kitchen timer, with seconds as well as minutes and with a loud bell, is essential. Set it for 1 minute less than the suggested time in the recipe, especially if you are unsure of your oven temperature – you can always increase the cooking time if needed.

TINS

Always select the correct size of tin, then wash and dry it carefully before you start. A good-quality heavy-duty tin should bake without scorching or warping in the heat of the oven, stay rust-free and last a lifetime.

Loaf tins are essential for making neat, brick-shaped breads. They're available in a variety of sizes – of these 450g (about 19 × 12.5 × 7.5cm) and 900g (about 26 × 12.5 × 7.5cm) are the most-used sizes. Heavy-duty tins won't dent or warp; silicone types won't give a good crisp crust and can be difficult to handle when filled with a heavy dough.

Heavy-duty roasting tin – put one on the oven floor to heat up when you turn on the oven, then fill it with a jug of cold water or ice cubes after you have loaded the dough into the oven to create a burst of steam, which helps give a crusty loaf (see page 23).

Springclip tins are deep metal tins with a spring release, a base that clamps in place when the clip is fastened, and a metal ring which lifts off when unclipped – they're mainly used for cake-making but are also useful for baking pull-apart rolls. They come in many sizes, with 20.5cm and 22–23cm tins being the most useful, but are not essential for bread-making.

WOODEN SPOON

These are invaluable and will last a lifetime. Wooden spoons are heat-resistant so are ideal for stirring mixtures over heat. It's a good idea to keep ones for baking separate from those that are used for savoury cooking, as they can absorb strong flavours.

Skills

Once your ingredients and equipment are lined up, you're ready to start baking some delicious bread!

The recipes in this book are designed to take you from absolute beginner to baking star, stage-by-stage. Some of the terms you'll find in the recipe methods are highlighted in bold, which means there's additional information about them in this section.

Below are in-depth explanations of the methods you'll use to get from flour, salt and water to a tasty loaf. Even confident bakers will be able to pick up some tips here so it's worth reading.

HOW TO MIX THE DOUGH

The key thing to think about when mixing dough is that you need to keep your yeast alive. Yeast is a simple living organism and is easily killed, by salt in particular. Many doughs raised by yeast also specify lukewarm milk or water in the recipe, and it's important that the liquid is not too hot or it could kill the yeast. After warming the liquid, check the temperature by dipping your little finger into it: it should feel just comfy – not too hot, not too cold. Once your weighed flour is in the bowl add the salt and any sugar before adding the yeast, so that the yeast doesn't come into direct contact with them. Now give it a stir to combine all the ingredients before adding the liquids and mixing it all together.

You can mix with a wooden spoon, your hand – using it like a paddle – or the dough hook attachment of a large free-standing food-mixer on the slowest speed. Use a dough scraper to get down to the bottom of the bowl, so that all your ingredients are fully incorporated (*see photo, left*).

HOW TO KNEAD

Thorough kneading is the key to successful bread-making: it ensures the yeast is evenly distributed so that your dough rises evenly and it develops the gluten in the flour. The stronger the flour (that is, the more protein it contains – this is stated on the pack, see page 11) the more gluten there is, and the more your dough is able to rise. Kneading develops the gluten from a tangled mass to a network of chains that stretch around the bubbles of carbon dioxide produced by the yeast.

Leave your mixed dough uncovered in its bowl for about 5 minutes before you start to knead and you'll find the kneading process easier because the flour will have had time to absorb the liquid properly. This makes a particular difference with wholemeal and rye flours, which often need more liquid than white flours, and are slower to hydrate. After this time you can judge whether or not the dough needs a little more flour or water, depending on the consistency specified in the recipe.

When kneading rye or wholemeal dough, give the dough (and yourself) a break: halfway through, cover your dough with an upturned bowl and have a rest for 5–10 minutes, then continue. Kneading in shorter bursts helps the gluten to gradually develop and strengthen – rye flour has very little gluten, which means it doesn't really become stretchy in the same way as a wheat flour dough.

How to knead by hand

1. Gather your dough mixture into a ball; it should be firm enough to leave the sides of the bowl clean. If necessary, work in a sprinkling of extra flour if the dough feels sticky, or a few dashes of liquid if there are dry crumbs.

2. Turn out your dough onto a very lightly floured or oiled worktop (unless otherwise stated in the recipe) and set a timer for 10 minutes.

3. Stretch your dough away from you by holding one end down with one hand and using the other hand to pull and stretch out the dough as if it were an elastic band (*see photo, right*). Gather the dough back into a ball. Give the ball a quarter turn.

4. Repeat these three movements over and over until your dough begins to change in texture and appearance to feel and look smooth, glossy and very pliable.

5. Shape your dough into a neat ball and leave to rise, as your recipe requires.

Knead using a free-standing food-mixer with a dough hook to reduce the kneading time – 4–5 minutes is best – and use the slowest possible speed *(see photo, left)*. Don't overwork the dough in the mixer – this is a real danger in food processors, which is why it's best to avoid using them for kneading – or you may over-extend the gluten and end up with a collapsing loaf with large holes in it. While it's impossible to over-knead by hand, always take care when using the food-mixer.

You'll also need to keep an eye out for under-kneading, which can produce a loaf that's soggy, flat or dense.

To test if the dough has been kneaded enough, take a small piece of dough, roughly the size of an egg, and stretch it between your fingers to make a thin, translucent sheet *(see photo, below left)*. If it doesn't stretch out, or it tears easily, then knead it for a little while longer.

HOW TO RISE AND PROVE THE DOUGH

Rising is the time when the yeast produces the bubbles of gas that cause the dough to rise and expand. Most recipes require the dough to rise until about double it's original size *(see photo, top right)*.

Yeast likes air (from kneading), food (from the flour, sugars or malt added to your dough), moisture (from the liquid in the dough, and in the atmosphere) and warmth. For the best results, bakers like to provide the dough with a moist and gently warm atmosphere (some build steamy proving tents, like mini greenhouses) as it's vital it doesn't dry out and form a skin (this is visible in the finished loaf as a dry or tough line running through it).

A room temperature of 20–24°C (68–75°F) is ideal for rising dough. If it is left in too hot a place, the yeast will grow too rapidly and the dough can become distorted and have a slight aftertaste. At cooler temperatures the yeast develops more slowly; some bakers prefer slower fermentation as it results in a richer flavour and a chewy crumb, so they mix the dough with cool or chilled water and leave it to rise in a cool place, or even the fridge, overnight. With some experimentation you can also slow the fermentation by using less yeast.

Proving is the name given to the last rising before baking, which happens after you've shaped the dough. Some breads only have one rising/proving stage, the Grant Loaf (page 54), for example – it was a wartime recipe that became very popular as it saved time for busy women, while breads with a really fine, cake-like texture have multiple rises so that the gas bubbles are repeatedly broken up and become smaller and smaller, such as Challah (page 138).

....

Check if the dough is sufficiently proved by looking at its size. After shaping, your dough needs to be left to rise and prove until it has around doubled in size. How long this takes will depend on the temperature of your dough (some doughs, such as brioche, are chilled before shaping) and how lively your dough is. If it's under-proved once it goes in the oven, it can suddenly expand in an unexpected way and become misshapen; if over-proved, your dough is likely to collapse in the oven as the gluten can't cope with all the gas bubbles. To test whether or not your dough is oven-ready, gently prod it (*see photo, right*): if it springs back, then it's not quite ready; if it returns to its original shape fairly slowly, or if there is a very slight

dent, then it's ready. A large dent means it is over-proved (although you can sometimes save the dough by gently kneading and reshaping, and carefully proving again).

HOW TO KNOCK BACK AND SHAPE A LOAF

All doughs must be knocked back before shaping, and gently kneaded to redistribute the gas bubbles. Knocking back breaks up the very large bubbles of gas within the dough so that you get smaller, finer bubbles that will rise more evenly.

Use your knuckles to punch down your risen, puffy dough so it collapses back to its original size (*see photo, left*); some bakers prefer to fold the dough over on itself two or three times.

Once shaped, all loaves need to be slashed with a sharp knife, or snipped with scissors, to help the loaf keep its shape as the gases expand in the oven. They are then left to prove before baking.

To make an oval loaf, form the knocked-back dough into an oval, then make a good crease in the dough lengthways along the centre using the edge of your hand (*see photo, left*). Roll the dough over to make a sausage shape (crease in the centre), then roll it onto the prepared baking tray so that the seam is underneath, the top is smooth and the loaf is evenly shaped. Slash or snip the top, cover and prove before baking.

To make a tin loaf, pat the knocked-back dough into a rectangle, with the shortest side the same length (not width) as the tin. (Make sure you don't use too much flour on the work surface or you may dry out the dough and create a gap in the centre when it bakes. Brush any excess flour away with a pastry brush.) Roll up the dough firmly, like a Swiss roll, pinch the long seam together well with your fingers and then put your dough into the tin, seam-side down, with the ends tucked under at each end (*see photo, right*). Your dough should fill roughly halfway up the tin. Slash or snip the top, cover and leave it to prove before baking.

To make a round loaf, gently knead your knocked-back dough into a ball shape. Roll the ball around under your cupped hand until it becomes smooth and neatly shaped. Set the ball on the prepared baking tray and snip or slash the top (*see photo, below right*), then cover and leave to prove before baking.

HOW TO BAKE A LOAF WITH A GOOD CRUST

Make sure your oven is thoroughly heated so the dough quickly puffs (known as the 'oven-spring') then sets, bakes evenly and forms a good crust. If you're worried about the oven temperature dropping dramatically as you load the bread into the oven you can heat it slightly higher than the recipe says and then turn it down to the specified temperature once the oven door is closed.

Creating a burst of steam in the oven at the start of baking will help give your loaf a crisp crust – the steam keeps the surface moist, helping the bread stretch easily; and once the surface has set, the moisture evaporates, leaving a crisp finish. To do this, put an empty roasting tin on the floor of the oven when you turn it on to heat up. Then, immediately after you've put your loaf in to bake, pour a jug of cold water, or add a handful of ice cubes, to the hot tin. Quickly close the oven door to trap the resulting steam inside.

To help give a good crisp bottom crust, put a strong baking sheet, baking stone or pizza stone into the oven when you turn it on to heat up and either slide your loaf directly onto it once shaped, or set the tin onto it. Lastly, and most importantly, make sure you bake your loaf thoroughly.

Glaze your bread to give it a deeper colour and, in some cases, added flavour. Bread is most often glazed with a beaten egg seasoned with a pinch of salt, but a glaze can be as simple as water, or more of a flavour feature, like olive oil and balsamic vinegar. Lightly brush the top of your bread and be careful not to glue it to any baking paper.

TO TEST IF THE BREAD IS DONE
Carefully remove the hot bread from the oven and turn it out, upside down, into one hand (with your all-important heavy-duty oven gloves on). Tap the underside of the loaf with your knuckles – if the bread sounds hollow, like a drum, then the loaf is cooked through (*see photo, left*); if you just get a dull 'thud', put the bread back into the oven, directly onto the oven shelf. Bake for a few more minutes, then test again. You'll find that a slightly over-baked loaf will taste far, far better than one that is under-baked.

TO COOL BAKED BREAD
Take it out of its tin (if using) and leave it to cool on a wire rack. If you leave it in the tin or on a baking sheet, the steam from the loaf will condense during cooling and turn the crust soggy. For a soft upper crust (for baps and sandwich bread, crumpets, muffins, etc.), cover or wrap the bakes loosely in a clean, dry tea towel or cloth, but never clingfilm (*see photo, right*).

HOW TO STORE BREAD

Once your bread is cold, cover it to prevent it becoming dry and stale. You can wrap it in a clean, dry tea towel or cloth and tuck it in a breadbox or container at room temperature, but not a sealed plastic container (you don't want the bread to start to sweat). Keep it away from warm kitchen lights and sunny shelves to stop the bread becoming warm and developing mould.

If you want to freeze the bread, wrap it tightly in clingfilm once cold, or store it in a freezer bag (or a sealed plastic container) for up to a month.

Help!

Sometimes things go wrong in the kitchen, no matter how experienced you are, but it's not a disaster! Here are some commonly encountered bread-making problems, and our expert suggestions as to how to resolve them.

WHY DIDN'T MY DOUGH RISE?

The most obvious reason is to do with the yeast. Check the expiry date – stale dried yeast will be ineffective (it doesn't last very long once opened and exposed to the air). If you used fresh yeast it may have passed its best or died, particularly if it was left unwrapped and exposed to the air, or left to dry out. (See page 13 for how to test to see if fresh yeast is alive.)

If the yeast was fresh and the dough still didn't rise, the yeast may have been killed as your dough was being made. Yeast is a tiny living organism and will die at temperatures much above blood temperature, so treat it carefully and check the temperature of the liquid you are using to mix the dough: dip in your little finger – if it feels a bit warm, replace some of the liquid with a cold version.

Whether you're using dried or fresh yeast, keep it away from direct contact with salt or sugar as these strong, concentrated ingredients will kill it. You could try mixing dried yeast in with the flour first, or crumble fresh yeast into a small bowl and mix it to a cream with a little of your lukewarm water or milk, and a very little sugar or flour (to feed it) before adding it to the flour.

If you used cold or chilled water to mix the dough and left it to rise in a cool spot, or used less yeast than specified in the recipe, the dough will be slower to rise (yeast thrives on gentle warmth), so be patient and move the dough to a warmer spot to encourage the yeast to grow. If it still doesn't budge, you'll have to throw it away and start again – but it's only flour and water!

WHY DID MY LOAF COLLAPSE IN THE OVEN?

It may have been left to prove (the final rising stage, see page 20) for too long, or in too warm a spot. If bread dough expands to more than double its original size, the gluten developed during kneading (see page 18), cannot expand any further to keep up with expansion of the bubbles of gas (from the yeast) and so eventually the structure breaks down and collapses in the heat of the oven.

When you first put a loaf into a hot oven it immediately starts to rise and expand – this is the 'oven spring', caused by the gas in the dough expanding. The high heat quickly kills off the yeast and starts to set the dough, but if the oven is too cool, the yeast keeps on producing bubbles of gas and the dough keeps on expanding until the gluten can't contain it and the dough collapses.

There's not much you can do: the loaf will taste fine but be a bit dense and heavy, so use it for toast or for making breadcrumbs.

WHY DOES MY BREAD SPREAD IN THE OVEN RATHER STAY IN A NEAT SHAPE?

Your dough may have been too soft when it was shaped, and needed more flour. Alternatively, your dough was very warm when it was shaped so it over-expanded (see above). If the dough feels too soft to hold a shape at the shaping stage it's a good idea to bake it in a tin. You can work in more flour but you risk ending up with a tough crumb.

THE CRUST IS SOFT, PALE AND SOGGY!

This happens if the oven temperature is too low, or the loaf hasn't been fully baked. Check the oven temperature is correct (double-check using an oven thermometer) and return the loaf to the hot oven – set it directly on the oven shelf (rather than in a tin or on a baking sheet) and bake it for a further 5–10 minutes. Test for 'doneness' by tapping on the underside of a loaf as it will sound hollow when fully baked. Brushing with glaze (see page 24) will help give a good brown crust next time.

WHY HAS MY LOAF CRACKED ALONG ONE SIDE?

If the loaf has risen unevenly, or has a crack to one side, it has probably been baked too far to one side of the oven, or too near a hot spot (you can use an oven thermometer to check for these). You can rotate the loaf a couple of times during baking so that it bakes evenly. Sometimes a loaf will crack along one side if you use the wrong tin for baking the dough – if the tin is too small for the quantity of dough, the dough will expand unevenly. The bread will still be perfectly good to eat, though.

WHY IS THERE A LARGE TUNNEL OR HOLE IN MY LOAF?

This is a very common problem, even for experienced bakers. It's usually caused by either under-kneading the dough so the gluten is not fully developed, or under-baking the loaf so the dough in the very centre didn't heat through and set, leaving a gap once cooled.

Sometimes a tin loaf has a distinct gap where the dough was rolled up (see page 22), caused by using too much flour

on the worktop, which dries the dough. Keep a clean and dry pastry brush at hand for brushing away the excess flour when shaping doughs. If this happens you can just cut around the hole and eat the rest of your delicious bread.

THE CRUST HAS BECOME DETACHED FROM THE CRUMB!

A 'flying crust' is another common problem, usually caused during shaping. When you roll up your dough for a tin loaf, make sure it is rolled tightly, with the seam pinched well with each roll (see page 23).

MY LOAF IS CRUMBLY AND DRY!

Usually this is because the dough was too dry (too much flour in proportion to the liquid) or the loaf was baked for too long and dried out in the oven. But you can use the loaf for breadcrumbs – once cold, freeze it tightly wrapped in clingfilm or stored in a freezer bag for up to one month.

WHY DOES MY LOAF TASTE YEASTY?

If you use too much yeast, the bread can have an unpleasant aftertaste (it also makes it become stale very quickly), but unfortunately there's nothing you can do after baking.

WHY IS MY LOAF DAMP?

If the crumb is damp, it wasn't baked for long enough – always test for doneness (see page 24). If the crumb is also very dense, the dough may not have been thoroughly kneaded (see page 18), so the gluten wasn't developed enough to form the structure of the loaf.

BAKE IT
BETTER
Recipes

Farmhouse White
Soda Bread

This yeast-free loaf is one of the easiest, quickest breads you can bake. Delicious toasted and spread with melting butter, or dunked into plates of steaming stew.

450g plain white flour, plus extra
for dusting
1 teaspoon bicarbonate of soda
1 teaspoon fine sea salt
about 350ml buttermilk

1. Preheat the oven to 220°C (200°C fan), 425°F, Gas 7. **Line** the baking sheet with baking paper. Sift the flour, bicarbonate of soda and sea salt into a mixing bowl, then make a little well in the middle.

2. Pour the buttermilk into the well and quickly **mix** it in with a round-bladed knife or your hands. Go gently here, don't overwork the dough or the finished loaf will be tough – stop mixing if the dough feels slightly sticky and looks rough and shaggy. If there are dry crumbs at the bottom of the bowl or the dough feels stiff or dry, work in a little more buttermilk (or milk or water) a tablespoon at a time; if the dough feels very sticky and clings to the sides of the bowl, work in a little more flour.

3. Lightly flour the worktop and your hands, then tip out the dough and **knead** it quickly – just 3 or 4 times – then **shape** it into a slightly craggy ball. Put the ball on the prepared baking sheet and dust it with flour. Cut a deep cross into the top with a sharp knife, then bake for about 35 minutes until the loaf is a good golden brown. You can **test** to see if the bread is cooked by tapping it on the base – it should sound hollow. **Cool** the loaf on a wire rack, then slice and eat the same day. It will still be quite fresh the next day, too, but after that it is best toasted.

Easy does it

HANDS-ON TIME:
10 minutes

HANDS-OFF TIME:
10 minutes

BAKING TIME:
35 minutes

MAKES:
1 medium loaf

SPECIAL
EQUIPMENT:
Baking sheet

STORAGE:
Best eaten the same
day or the next day

Simple Crusty
White Loaf

You can't beat a good old-fashioned crusty loaf. This recipe uses a handful of ingredients, but once you've made this you'll be experimenting with all sorts of flavours and ingredients.

700g strong white bread flour, plus extra for dusting
10g fine sea salt
7g sachet fast-action dried yeast
about 450ml lukewarm water

1. Put the flour and sea salt into a large mixing bowl or the bowl of a food-mixer and **mix** thoroughly with your hands or use the dough hook attachment set on the slowest speed. Mix in the dried yeast, then make a well in the middle.

2. Pour the lukewarm water into the well, then gradually mix the flour at the sides into the water with your hand or the dough hook (still on the slowest speed), mixing it together until it makes a soft but not sticky dough. If there are dry crumbs at the bottom of the bowl or the dough feels stiff or dry, work in a little more lukewarm water a tablespoon at a time; if the dough feels very sticky and clings to the sides of the bowl, work in some more flour.

3. Tip out the dough onto a lightly floured worktop and **knead** it well with your hands for 10 minutes, or for 4 minutes with the dough hook on the slowest speed. You will see the texture and appearance of the dough change as you knead it; it will feel pliable and stretchy but it should still be firm enough to keep its shape. If the dough has been kneaded enough it will look smooth and silky; to **test** it, when you

stretch a small piece it should look like a translucent sheet.

4. Put the dough back in the bowl and cover the bowl tightly with clingfilm or a snap-on lid, or pop it into a large plastic bag and close tightly. Leave to **rise** on the worktop until it has doubled in size: this may take about 1 hour in a warmish kitchen, 2 hours at normal room temperature, 3 hours in a cool room, or overnight in the fridge. *Continued*

Try Something Different

If you want a more crunchy texture, add 2 tbsp sesame seeds to the flour along with the salt. Follow the recipe up to step 8 then uncover the loaves and brush them with beaten egg. Sprinkle with some more seeds then slash the loaves and bake as above.

HANDS-ON TIME:
27–32 minutes

HANDS-OFF TIME:
2–4 hours or overnight + 1 hour

BAKING TIME:
35 minutes

MAKES:
2 medium loaves

SPECIAL EQUIPMENT:
1–2 baking sheets; Roasting tin

STORAGE:
Once cold, wrap in clingfilm or pop into freezer bags and freeze for up to 1 month

5. When the dough is ready, uncover the bowl and punch down (**knock back**) the dough with your knuckles to deflate it. Tip it out onto a lightly floured worktop and knead it gently for a minute to spread the bubbles of gas evenly through the loaf – this will give the loaf an even crumb and stops holes developing. Divide the dough into two equal pieces, either by eye, or weigh it if you want to be more accurate.

6. **Shape** each piece of dough into a ball, then cup your hand and roll one ball on the worktop for a minute until it forms a neat shape and is very smooth. Put it on a sheet of baking paper while you do the same with the other ball of dough.

7. Dust both balls with flour, then cover them lightly with clingfilm. Leave to **prove** and rise on the worktop for about 1 hour at normal room temperature until they have just doubled in size.

8. Towards the end of the proving time, preheat the oven to 230°C (210°C fan), 450°F, Gas 8. Put one or two baking sheets into the oven to heat up – you may be able to fit both loaves onto one sheet – and put a roasting tin in the bottom of the oven to heat up.

9. Uncover the risen loaves and sprinkle them with a little more flour, then slash the top of each fairly deeply with a sharp knife. Very carefully lift the baking paper, loaves and all, onto the very hot baking sheet or sheets and put them straight into the oven. For a really good **crust,** quickly pour a jug of cold water or add ice cubes to the hot roasting tin on the bottom of the oven. This will create a burst of steam, so immediately close the door. Let the loaf bake for 15 minutes, without opening the oven door.

10. After 15 minutes, take the sheet or sheets out of the oven, turn them round, then put them back in the oven to help them brown evenly on all sides. Turn down the oven to 200°C (180°C fan), 400°F, Gas 6 and bake for another 17–20 minutes or until the loaves are a really good golden brown. **Test** the loaves are cooked by tapping them on the base – they should sound hollow.

11. Put the loaves on a wire rack to **cool** before **storing**. Eat within 5 days.

Soft-crust
Sandwich Bread

This really is the best thing since sliced bread. This loaf has three secret ingredients: milk and butter give it a soft crumb, while golden syrup makes it less crumbly and easier to slice.

about 325ml milk
25g unsalted butter
1 teaspoon golden syrup
500g strong white bread flour, plus extra for dusting
7g fine sea salt
7g sachet fast-action dried yeast

To finish
small knob of unsalted butter

HANDS-ON TIME:
30 minutes

HANDS-OFF TIME:
2 hours

BAKING TIME:
35 minutes

MAKES:
1 medium loaf

SPECIAL EQUIPMENT:
900g loaf tin (about 26 × 12.5 × 7.5cm)

STORAGE:
Once cold, wrap in clingfilm or pop into freezer bags and freeze for up to 1 month

1. Pour the milk into a small saucepan, add the butter and golden syrup, and heat gently to melt the butter. Give it a stir, then take the pan off the heat and let it cool until the liquid feels just warm when you dip in your little finger.

2. Put the flour and sea salt into a mixing bowl or the bowl of a food-mixer and **mix** well with your hands or the dough hook attachment. Mix in the dried yeast then make a well in the centre.

3. Pour the lukewarm milk mixture into the well and mix everything together with your hand or the dough hook on the slowest speed to make a soft dough. If the dough feels stiff or dry or there are some stray dry crumbs at the bottom of the bowl, work in a little more lukewarm milk, a tablespoon at a time; if the dough feels very sticky and clings to the sides of the bowl, work in a little more flour. Leave the soft dough in the bowl, uncovered, for 5 minutes so that the flour can fully hydrate, which will make it easier to work.

4. Lightly flour the worktop and your fingers, then tip out the dough and **knead** it really well for 10 minutes, or for 5 minutes in a mixer with the dough hook on the slowest speed. The dough should feel slightly firmer, silky-smooth, very elastic and pliable. Put the dough back in the bowl, then cover the bowl tightly with clingfilm or a snap-on lid, or pop it into a large plastic bag and close tightly. Leave to **rise** on the worktop for about 1 hour at normal room temperature until it has doubled in size. Grease the inside and the rim of the tin with butter.

Continued

5. Punch down (**knock back**) the risen dough with your knuckles to deflate it, then tip it out onto the lightly floured worktop. Knead it a couple of times to even it out and shift any large air bubbles, then dust your fingers with flour and firmly press it out to a 26 × 30cm rectangle of an even thickness. Roll up the dough fairly tightly from one short end – a bit like a Swiss roll – pinching the dough together as you go.

6. When it is all rolled up, pinch the seam firmly. Put the bread seam-side down, tuck the ends under the roll and push the loaf into the tin.

7. Gently press your hand down flat on top of the dough to push it right into the corners of the tin and flatten it on the surface. This will give the baked loaf a neat, fairly brick-like shape (or just slightly rounded) instead of the usual well-domed crust. Slip the tin into a large plastic bag, letting in some air so the plastic doesn't stick to the dough, and close tightly. Leave the dough to **prove** and rise at normal room temperature for about 1 hour until doubled in size.

8. Towards the end of the proving time, preheat the oven to 220°C (200°C fan), 425°F, Gas 7. Take the tin out of the bag and bake it for 15 minutes, then reduce the oven temperature to 180°C (160°C fan), 350°F, Gas 4 and bake for 20 minutes until the loaf is a good golden brown. To **test** if is the bread is done, turn it out and tap it on the base with your knuckles – if it sounds hollow it is ready, but if there's a dull 'thud', put it back in the tin and pop it in the oven for another 5 minutes, then test again.

9. Turn out the cooked loaf onto a wire rack, then quickly rub a knob of unsalted butter over the top using an old butter wrapper or piece of kitchen paper. Leave the bread to **cool** until completely cold before storing. Eat within 5 days – after that it is best toasted.

Simple Spelt Loaf

This 'loaf' is made from balls of dough pressed together like a caterpillar – which might encourage children to eat this nutritious bread. The flavour is even better a day or two after baking.

700g stoneground wholegrain spelt flour, plus extra for dusting
10g fine sea salt
7g sachet fast-action dried yeast
25g unsalted butter, melted
1 tablespoon soft-set honey
about 475ml lukewarm water

HANDS-ON TIME:
20 minutes

HANDS-OFF TIME:
1¾–2 hours
+ 5 minutes

BAKING TIME:
35 minutes

MAKES:
1 large loaf

SPECIAL EQUIPMENT:
Baking sheet

STORAGE:
Once cold, wrap in clingfilm or pop into freezer bags and freeze for up to 1 month

1. Put the spelt flour into a large mixing bowl or the bowl of a food-mixer with the sea salt and **mix** in with your hand or the dough hook attachment. Mix in the dried yeast and make a well in the middle.

2. Pour the butter and the soft-set honey into the well, then add the lukewarm water and mix everything together with your hand or the dough hook attachment on the slowest speed. If the dough feels stiff or dry or there are some stray dry crumbs at the bottom of the bowl, work in a little more water, a tablespoon at a time; if the dough feels very sticky and clings to the sides of the bowl, work in more flour. Once the dough comes together into a ball, leave it in the bowl, uncovered, for 5 minutes to let the flour fully hydrate – this will make it easier to knead. The dough should feel soft but not sticky, but if not, add a little flour or water to get the right texture.

3. Lightly flour the worktop, then tip out the dough and **knead** it thoroughly for 10 minutes, or 5 minutes using the dough hook on the slowest speed. The dough should feel very elastic and pliable. Put the dough back in the bowl and cover the bowl tightly with clingfilm or a snap-on lid, or pop it into a large plastic bag and close tightly. Put the bowl somewhere warm and leave the dough to **rise** for about 1 hour until doubled in size. Line the baking sheet with baking paper.

Continued

Try Something Different

For an extra nutty crunch, replace the melted butter with 2 tbsp walnut or hazelnut oil, then add 200g walnut halves or blanched hazelnuts (toasted, cooled and halved) to the dough at the end of the kneading time. Knead for another minute or so until evenly distributed, then follow the recipe. You could also bake the loaf in a tin – just grease a 900g loaf tin (about 26 × 12.5 × 7.5cm) with butter and shape the dough to fit it (see Breakfast Loaf on page 76 for details). Leave the dough to rise, then bake and test for 'doneness' as in the recipe here, allowing 35–40 minutes' baking time.

4. Punch down (**knock back**) the risen dough with your knuckles to deflate it, then turn it out onto a lightly floured worktop. Knead it gently for a minute, then dust your hands with flour and shape the dough into a fat sausage, 35cm long. Using a sharp knife or dough scraper, cut the sausage into 5 × 7cm portions.

5. **Shape** each portion into a neat ball, then put them on the baking sheet, pressing them together like the sections in a caterpillar. Sprinkle with a little flour, then cover lightly with clingfilm or slip the baking sheet into a large plastic bag, letting in some air so that the plastic doesn't stick to the dough, and close tightly. Leave to **prove** and rise for 45–60 minutes until doubled in size. Towards the end of the proving time, preheat the oven to 200°C (180°C fan), 400°F, Gas 6.

6. Uncover the loaf and bake for about 35 minutes. **Test** the bread is cooked by tapping the base – it should sound hollow. If there's a dull 'thud', pop the loaf back in the oven and bake for another 5 minutes, then test again. Turn out onto a wire rack and leave to **cool** completely before storing. Eat within 5 days, but after that it is best toasted.

Cornbread

With no yeast, no kneading or rising required, this spicy cornbread can be on the table in half an hour. If you like, add 3 tablespoons toasted pine nuts, corn kernels or grated cheese.

140g yellow cornmeal
125g plain flour
½ teaspoon fine sea salt
1½ teaspoons baking powder
½ teaspoon bicarbonate of soda
1 medium-hot green chilli pepper, or to taste, deseeded and finely chopped
1 medium egg

50g unsalted butter, melted
1½ tablespoons maple syrup or soft-set honey
225ml buttermilk

1. Preheat the oven to 200°C (180°C fan), 400°F, Gas 6. Grease the inside and rim of the tin with butter.

2. Put the cornmeal, flour, sea salt, baking powder and bicarbonate of soda into a large bowl with the chopped chilli and **mix** it all together with a wooden spoon.

3. Break the egg into a separate bowl or jug and pour it over the melted butter and maple syrup or soft-set honey. Beat everything together with a fork and tip it into the cornmeal mixture. Give it a good stir to make a thick, smooth batter.

4. Scrape all the mixture into the prepared tin, spreading it out evenly. Bake for 18–20 minutes until golden brown and a skewer poked into the middle of the bread comes out clean with no crumbs on it.

5. Turn out the cornbread onto a board and cut it into large squares. It's best eaten warm as soon as possible, or at least on the same day.

Easy does it

HANDS-ON TIME:
10 minutes

BAKING TIME:
18–20 minutes

MAKES:
1 medium bread

SPECIAL EQUIPMENT:
20cm square cake tin

STORAGE:
This needs to be eaten on the day you make it

Easy No-knead Cheese Loaf

This rich, brioche-like cheese bread is made with just one rise in the tin. You can swap the Gruyère for Comté or Emmental; or scatter with 25g grated cheese before baking for extra crunch.

HANDS-ON TIME:
15 minutes

BAKING TIME:
40–45 minutes

MAKES:
1 large loaf

SPECIAL
EQUIPMENT:
900g loaf tin (about
26 × 12.5 × 7.5cm)

STORAGE:
Once cold, wrap
in clingfilm or pop
into freezer bags and
freeze for up to
1 month

500g strong white bread flour
7g fine sea salt
1/4 teaspoon English mustard powder
1/4 teaspoon dried chilli flakes,
or to taste
7g sachet fast-action dried yeast

100g grated Gruyère cheese
about 250ml milk, at room
temperature
4 medium eggs, at room temperature

1. Grease the tin with butter. Put the bread flour, sea salt, English mustard powder and dried chilli flakes into a large mixing bowl. **Mix** well with your hands, then mix in the dried yeast.

2. Scatter the Gruyère over the flour and gently stir it in so there are no clumps and it is evenly mixed through. If you find the bowl slips, stand it on a damp tea towel.

3. Put the milk into a jug and break in the eggs, then beat them together with a fork. Pour this into the flour mixture and mix everything together with your hands to make a soft and sticky dough.

4. Now, using your hand as a paddle, beat and slap the dough in the bowl for 3–4 minutes until it feels very stretchy and elastic.

5. Scrape the dough out of the bowl and into the prepared tin, pressing it into the corners so that it neatly fills all the spaces. Slip the tin into a large plastic bag, then let in some air so the plastic doesn't stick to the dough and close tightly.

6. Leave the tin on the worktop to **rise** at normal room temperature for 2–2½ hours until the dough has puffed up to 1cm below the rim of the tin.

7. Towards the end of the rising time, preheat the oven to 190°C (170°C fan), 375°F, Gas 5.

8. Remove the tin from the bag and bake for 40–45 minutes until the loaf is a good golden brown. To **test** if the loaf is ready, turn it out and tap the base: if it sounds hollow, it is done; if there's a dull 'thud', put the loaf back in the oven on the shelf (you don't need to put it back in the tin) for another 5 minutes, then test again. **Cool** the loaf on a wire rack before storing. Eat within 5 days, but after that it is best toasted.

Shaped Bread Rolls

You can cater for all tastes with these bread rolls. Poppy seeds and sesame seeds will add a wow factor to a humble bread roll, or you could try oatmeal, porridge oats or wheat flakes.

HANDS-ON TIME:
40 minutes

HANDS-OFF TIME:
4¾–7 hours or
overnight
+ 45–60 minutes

BAKING TIME:
17–25 minutes

MAKES:
24 bread rolls

SPECIAL
EQUIPMENT:
2 baking sheets;
Roasting tin

STORAGE:
Once cold, wrap
in clingfilm or pop
into freezer bags and
freeze for up to
1 month

1.5kg strong white bread flour,
plus extra for dusting
2 × 7g sachets fast-action dried yeast
900ml lukewarm water
25g fine sea salt

For sprinkling
sesame seeds/poppy seeds/nigella
(black onion seeds)/oatmeal
porridge oats/wheat flakes/grated
cheese (your choice or optional)

To finish
1 egg beaten with a pinch of salt,
to glaze, or water

1. Put 1kg of the flour into a large mixing bowl or the bowl of a food-mixer and add one of the sachets dried yeast. **Mix** everything together with your hand or the dough hook attachment. Pour in 600ml lukewarm water and mix again with your hand or the dough hook on the slowest speed to make a soft but not sticky dough. If the dough feels stiff or dry or there are some stray dry crumbs at the bottom of the bowl, work in a little more water, a tablespoon at a time; if the dough feels very sticky and clings to the sides of the bowl, work in a little more flour.

2. Lightly flour the worktop and turn out the dough. **Knead** it for about 10 minutes or for 5 minutes in the food-mixer using the dough hook on the slowest speed. The dough should feel slightly firmer but very smooth and elastic.

3. Put the dough back in the bowl and cover the bowl tightly with clingfilm or a snap-on lid, or pop it into a large plastic bag and close tightly. Leave for at least 4 hours but no more than 6 hours at normal room temperature, or you can put it in the fridge overnight. The dough will puff up then slightly collapse – that's normal!

Continued

Try Something Different

To turn half the dough into a large loaf, at Step 6, pat out the dough to a rectangle 3cm thick and 30cm long. Fold in both short ends by about 4cm, then roll up the dough fairly tightly from one long side like a Swiss roll, pinching it at every roll and pinching the final seam. Put seam-side down on a lined baking sheet and leave it to rise. Just before baking, brush the top with water or beaten egg, then sprinkle with seeds and slash the top several times. Bake for 35–40 minutes.

4. For the next stage, mix 450g of the remaining 500g flour with the sea salt in a mixing bowl using your hand or in the bowl of the food-mixer using the dough hook. Stir in the second sachet dried yeast, pour in 300ml lukewarm water and mix everything together with your hand or the dough hook on the slowest speed to make a fairly firm dough.

5. Lightly flour the worktop, turn out both doughs onto it and **knead** them together for about 5 minutes, or put them both into the food-mixer bowl and knead for 3–4 minutes using the dough hook on the slowest speed until they are well combined. When you handle the dough it should feel smooth and pliable but also fairly firm so it can hold its shape. Cover the dough lightly with clingfilm and leave on the worktop to rest for 15 minutes. **Line** the baking sheets with baking paper.

6. To **shape** the rolls, weigh the dough and divide it into 24 equal portions.

7. If you want to make round rolls, shape each portion into a neat ball, then gently roll it around on the worktop under your cupped hand for a few seconds until it is smooth and round.

8. If you want to make finger rolls, shape each portion into a ball, then roll it with your hands on the worktop to a neat sausage about 16cm long with tapering ends.

9. If you're feeling confident and creative, try making plaits. Flatten each portion into a rectangle about 7.5 × 15cm, then cut it into three lengthways, leaving the dough attached at one end, and plait the three strands together. Tuck the ends under neatly when you've finished the plait.

10. Knots are slightly easier than plaits; shape each portion into a neat sausage about 20cm long, then gently tie it into a simple knot. You can leave the ends free or tuck them in or under the dough. Whatever shape you have made, arrange the rolls on the lined baking sheets spaced well apart.

11. Slip each sheet into a large plastic bag, letting in some air so that the plastic doesn't stick to the dough, and close tightly. Leave to **rise** for 30–45 minutes (or a little longer if the first dough was left in the fridge) at normal room temperature until almost doubled in size.

12. Towards the end of the rising time, preheat the oven to 220°C (200°C fan), 425°F, Gas 7 and put a roasting tin in the bottom of the oven to heat up.

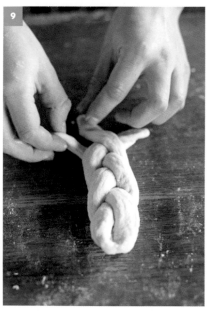

13. When the rolls are ready to bake, uncover them and brush them lightly with the 1 egg beaten with a pinch of salt, or water. If you are using egg glaze, be careful not to 'glue' the dough to the baking paper. If you are adding a topping, sprinkle it over now.

14. If you are making round rolls, cut a deep cross in the top of each and for finger rolls, slash the length of each roll.

14

15. Slide the sheets into the oven, then quickly pour a jug of cold water or add ice cubes to the hot roasting tin to create a burst of steam. Close the door immediately to keep in the steam and help give the rolls a really good **crust**. Bake for 17–25 minutes, depending on the shape, until they are golden brown.

16. Put the rolls on a wire rack to **cool,** then **store** when completely cold. Eat within 5 days, but after that they are best toasted.

Grant Loaf

With no kneading required, this is simple as it gets. Use top-quality stoneground wholegrain spelt flour for the best flavour. Swap the sesame seeds for oatmeal or spelt flakes.

750g stoneground wholegrain spelt flour suitable for breadmaking
10g fine sea salt
15g unsalted butter, diced
7g sachet fast-action dried yeast
1 rounded teaspoon soft-set honey
650ml lukewarm water
1 tablespoon sesame seeds, for sprinkling

HANDS-ON TIME:
10 minutes

HANDS-OFF TIME:
45–60 minutes

BAKING TIME:
45 minutes

MAKES:
1 large loaf

SPECIAL EQUIPMENT:
900g loaf tin (about 26 × 12.5 × 7.5cm)

STORAGE:
Once cold, wrap in clingfilm or pop into freezer bags and freeze for up to 1 month

1. Grease the inside and the rim of the tin with butter. Put the spelt flour and sea salt into a large mixing bowl and **mix** well with your hand. Rub the butter into the flour with the tips of your fingers until you can't see any lumps and the mixture looks like fine crumbs. Mix in the dried yeast and make a well in the middle.

2. Stir the soft-set honey into the lukewarm water, then pour into the well. Using your hand, tip the flour a little at a time into the water and mix to make a soft, sticky dough. Beat the dough vigorously in the bowl with your hand, taking it from the sides and working it into the middle, until it feels elastic and slippery – it will be wetter than usual dough. Mix for about 5 minutes until it comes away from the sides of the bowl, leaving them clean.

3. Tip the dough into the prepared tin and with wet fingers gently ease it into the corners to evenly fill the tin.

4. Cover the tin with a damp tea towel or pop it into a large plastic bag and let in some air so that the plastic doesn't stick to the dough, and close tightly. Leave to **rise** in a slightly warm but not hot place for 45–60 minutes until the dough has risen almost to the top of the tin. (If the dough rises very quickly it will get holes in the middle of the baked loaf – if it's a hot day, use water from the cold tap in the recipe.) Towards the end of the rising time, preheat the oven to 200°C (180°C fan), 400°F, Gas 6.

5. Uncover the dough and sprinkle over the sesame seeds, then bake for 45 minutes until it is a good golden brown. **Test** the bread is done by giving it a tap on the base – if it sounds hollow like a drum it is ready, but if there's a dull 'thud', put it back in the oven on the shelf (you don't need to put it back in the tin) for a further 5 minutes, then test again. **Cool** on a wire rack then **store**. Eat within 4 days, but after that it is best toasted.

Hearty Mixed Grain Loaf

The perfect accompaniment to smoked fish, creamy cheeses or sharp jams. Rye flour has a distinctive flavour, but adding nutty-tasting spelt and white flour makes it a lighter loaf.

200g stoneground wholegrain rye flour
200g stoneground wholegrain spelt flour
200g strong white bread flour, plus extra for dusting

10g fine sea salt
7g sachet fast-action dried yeast
1 tablespoon black treacle
1 tablespoon plain yoghurt (unsweetened)
about 375ml lukewarm water

1. Put the rye flour, spelt flour and bread flour into a large mixing bowl or the bowl of a food-mixer, add the sea salt and **mix** with your hand or the dough hook attachment until thoroughly combined. Mix the dried yeast into the flour and make a well in the middle.

2. Mix the black treacle, yoghurt and lukewarm water together in a jug and pour this into the well. Gradually work the flours into the liquid using your hand or the dough hook attachment on a food-mixer set on the slowest speed to make a very soft dough – the rye flour will make it feel very sticky. If the dough feels stiff or dry or there are some stray dry crumbs at the bottom of the bowl, work in a little more lukewarm water, a tablespoon at a time; if the dough feels very sticky and clings to the sides of the bowl, work in a little more white bread flour.

3. Once you've mixed in all the flour, cover the bowl with clingfilm, a snap-on lid or a damp tea towel and leave it for 10 minutes – this will help the flours hydrate and absorb the liquid, which will make the dough easier to knead.

4. Turn out the dough onto a lightly floured worktop and **knead** thoroughly by hand for 12 minutes, or 5 minutes using the dough hook on the slowest speed, until the dough feels slightly firmer, stretchy and pliable – it will feel stickier than a white flour dough.

5. Put the dough back in the bowl and cover the bowl tightly with clingfilm or a snap-on lid, or pop it into a large plastic bag and close tightly. Leave on the worktop to **rise** for about 1 hour (in a warm kitchen) or 1½ hours (at room temperature) until doubled in size. Rye flour is a little more fussy than other flours, needing more TLC to get going – it prefers warmth and moisture, so don't leave it in the fridge to rise or you'll get a heavy dough. Line the baking sheet with baking paper.
Continued

Easy does it

HANDS-ON TIME:
30 minutes

HANDS-OFF TIME:
2–2½ hours
+ 10 minutes

BAKING TIME:
35–40 minutes

MAKES:
1 medium loaf

SPECIAL EQUIPMENT:
Baking sheet

STORAGE:
Once cold, wrap in clingfilm or pop into freezer bags and freeze for up to 1 month

6. Punch down (**knock back**) the risen dough to deflate it, then turn it out onto a lightly floured worktop. Knead it very gently for a minute to even out the dough and break up any air bubbles. To **shape** the ball into a neat oval, gently knead the dough into an oval about 20cm long. Make a good crease lengthways along the centre of the dough using the side of your hand.

7. Roll the dough onto its side to make a two-layer sausage shape, then roll it over again so the seam is underneath and the top looks smooth and even-shaped.

8. Put the loaf, seam-side down, onto the prepared baking sheet.

9. Slash the top diagonally a few times with a sharp knife, then slip the baking sheet into a large plastic bag, letting in some air so that the plastic doesn't stick to the dough and close tightly, or cover loosely with clingfilm. Leave to **prove** and rise for about 1 hour until doubled in size.

10. Towards the end of the rising time, preheat the oven to 220°C (200°C fan), 425°F, Gas 7. When the loaf is ready, uncover it and sprinkle it with a little flour, then bake for 15 minutes. Reduce the oven temperature to 190°C (170°C fan), 375°F, Gas 5 and bake for a further 20–25 minutes. **Test** the bread is done by giving it a tap on the base – if it sounds hollow like a drum it is ready, but if there's a dull 'thud', put it back in the oven on the shelf (you don't need to put it back in the tin) for a further 5 minutes, then test again. **Cool** on a wire rack then **store**. Eat within 5 days, but after that it is best toasted.

Walnut Roquefort Loaf

Now you've got the hang of the basics it's time to experiment with flavour. This is the perfect loaf to try something different, dotted through with tangy Roquefort and crunchy walnuts.

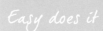

Easy does it

HANDS-ON TIME:
30 minutes

HANDS-OFF TIME:
2½–2¾ hours

BAKING TIME:
25 minutes

MAKES:
2 medium loaves

SPECIAL EQUIPMENT:
Baking sheet;
Roasting tin

STORAGE:
Once cold, wrap in clingfilm or pop into freezer bags and freeze for up to 1 month

100g walnut pieces
350g strong white bread flour, plus extra for dusting
150g white spelt flour suitable for breadmaking
8g fine sea salt
7g sachet fast-action dried yeast
150g Roquefort cheese, at room temperature
about 325ml water, at room temperature

1. Heat the oven to 180°C (160°C fan), 350°F, Gas 4. Tip the walnut pieces into an ovenproof dish and toast in the oven for 7–10 minutes until lightly coloured. Leave to cool and turn off the oven for now.

2. Put the bread flour and spelt flour into a large mixing bowl, add the sea salt and **mix** really well. Sprinkle the dried yeast into the bowl and mix it through. Crumble in the Roquefort with the cooled walnut pieces, then give everything a good stir with your hand. Make a well in the middle.

3. Pour the room-temperature water into the well and mix everything together with your hand to make a soft dough. If the dough feels stiff or dry or there are some stray dry crumbs at the bottom of the bowl, work in a little more water, a tablespoon at a time; if the dough feels very sticky and clings to the sides of the bowl, work in a little more flour.

4. Dust the worktop and your hands with flour, then turn out the dough. **Knead** it very gently for a couple of minutes – the cheese will start to break up, so go gently and don't work the dough too much or it will become greasy. Put the dough back in the mixing bowl and cover the bowl tightly with clingfilm or a snap-on lid and leave on the worktop to **rise** for 1 hour. You want the dough to look puffy. Line the baking sheet with baking paper.
Continued

Try Something Different

You could replace the walnuts with pecan halves for a slightly sweeter taste, but watch them carefully as you toast them because they brown quickly. For a richer, more intense flavour, you could use Stilton instead of Roquefort.

5. Dust the worktop and your hands with flour. Turn out the dough and knead gently for 5 minutes, this time the dough should feel stretchy and elastic. Pop the dough back in the bowl, cover and leave just as before for 45–60 minutes until doubled in size. Turn out the dough onto the lightly floured worktop again and divide it in half – you can do this by eye, or you can weigh it out to be really precise. Using your hands, pat out each piece of dough into a rectangle 15 × 20cm. Roll each one up tightly from one short side, then pinch the seam to seal.

6. Move one roll of dough to an unfloured part of the worktop and, with your hands, gently roll it back and forth to make a neat, fat sausage-shaped loaf 30cm long with tapered ends.

7. Put this seam-side down on the prepared baking sheet, then repeat with the second roll and put it on the baking sheet well apart from the other one to allow it to expand. Cover loosely with clingfilm or a dry tea towel and leave to **prove** and **rise** on the worktop for about 45 minutes until doubled in size.

8. Towards the end of the proving time, preheat the oven to 220°C (200°C fan), 425°F, Gas 7. Put a roasting tin in the bottom of the oven to heat up. Uncover the risen loaves and brush them lightly with water. Slash each loaf diagonally several times with a sharp knife, then put them into the oven. Quickly pour a jug of cold water or add ice cubes to the hot roasting tin to create a burst of steam, then immediately close the door. This will help create a good **crust**. Bake for about 25 minutes until the loaves are a rich golden brown. To **test** if the loaves are done, tap their bases — if they sound hollow, transfer them to a wire rack to cool, but if there's a dull 'thud', put them back in the oven for another 5 minutes and test again. **Cool** on a wire rack then **store**. Eat the same day or the next day.

Pull-apart
Buttermilk Rolls

Buttermilk gives these delicious fluffy white bread rolls a little tang. These are really easy to make but look so professional, especially when topped with sesame or poppy seeds.

750g white bread flour, plus extra for dusting
10g fine sea salt
7g sachet fast-action dried yeast
about 550ml buttermilk, at room temperature

For the glaze
1 egg beaten with 1 teaspoon water
1–2 tablespoons oatmeal, sesame seeds, poppy seeds or wheat flakes

1. Put the bread flour and sea salt into a large mixing bowl or the bowl of a food-mixer and **mix** thoroughly with your hand or the dough hook attachment. Sprinkle over and stir in the dried yeast.

2. Pour the buttermilk into the bowl and gradually work the flour into the liquid with your hand or the dough hook on the slowest speed to make a fairly soft and slightly sticky dough. It will feel heavy compared to simple white bread doughs, but don't worry, it will lighten up on baking! If the dough feels stiff or dry or there are some stray dry crumbs at the bottom of the bowl, work in a little more buttermilk (or water), a tablespoon at a time; if the dough feels very sticky and clings to the sides of the bowl, work in a little more flour. Leave the dough in the bowl, uncovered, for 5 minutes to help the flour fully hydrate and make the dough easier to knead.

3. Turn the dough out onto a lightly floured worktop and **knead** it well for 10 minutes until fairly firm but very smooth and elastic, or use the dough hook in a food-mixer set to the slowest speed for 4 minutes.

4. Put the dough back in the bowl then cover the bowl tightly with clingfilm or a snap-on lid, or pop the bowl into a large plastic bag and close it tightly. Leave on the worktop to **rise** for 1½ hours until it has doubled in size. Grease the tin or baking sheet with butter.
Continued

Easy does it

HANDS-ON TIME:
35 minutes

HANDS-OFF TIME:
2–2 hours
10 minutes

BAKING TIME:
35 minutes

MAKES:
15 rolls

SPECIAL EQUIPMENT:
Large round baking tin (about 26–30cm across), or roasting tin, or baking sheet

STORAGE:
Once cold, wrap in clingfilm or pop into freezer bags and freeze for up to 1 month

5. Uncover the dough and punch it down (**knock back**) to deflate it, then tip it out onto a lightly floured worktop. Weigh the dough and then divide it into 15 equal portions. **Shape** each piece into a ball with your hands then, one at a time, cup your hand over one ball and roll it around on the worktop for a few seconds. Put the ball in the prepared tin.

6. Repeat with all the other balls, neatly arranging them in the tin so that they gently touch. Cover the tin with clingfilm or slip it into a large plastic bag and close tightly. Leave to **prove** and rise on the worktop for 30–40 minutes until almost doubled in size.

7. Towards the end of the proving time, preheat the oven to 220°C (200°C fan), 425°F, Gas 7.

8. Uncover the rolls and brush them lightly with the 1 egg beaten with 1 teaspoon of water, then sprinkle over the 1–2 tablespoons of oatmeal, sesame or poppy seeds or wheat flakes.

9. Bake for about 35 minutes until the rolls are a good golden brown and firm to the touch. Check them after 25 minutes and turn the tin if necessary so that all the rolls take on an even colour. Tip the rolls onto a wire rack in one cluster, so that they are ready to serve in one piece. Eat warm from the oven or on the day of baking.

Cottage Loaf

The classic English loaf, with a twist. Here spelt flour adds an old-fashioned flavour, but if you prefer you can use white flour or swap out 100g of spelt with wholemeal flour.

675g white spelt flour suitable for breadmaking, plus extra for dusting
10g fine sea salt
15g unsalted butter, diced
7g sachet fast-action dried yeast
about 400ml water, at room temperature
1 medium egg beaten with a pinch of salt, to glaze

Easy does it

HANDS-ON TIME:
30 minutes

HANDS-OFF TIME:
about 2¼ hours

BAKING TIME:
35–40 minutes

MAKES:
1 large loaf

SPECIAL EQUIPMENT:
Large baking sheet; Roasting tin

STORAGE:
Once cold, wrap in clingfilm or pop into freezer bags and freeze for up to 1 month

1. Put the spelt flour and sea salt into a large mixing bowl or the bowl of a food-mixer and **mix** well with your hand or the dough hook attachment. Rub in the butter with the tips of your fingers until the mixture looks like fine crumbs. Stir in the dried yeast, mixing well with your hand or the dough hook, then make a well in the centre.

2. Pour the room-temperature water into the well, then gradually work the flour into the water with your hand or the dough hook on the slowest speed to make a fairly firm dough. The texture of the dough is important; if it's too soft it won't hold its shape so it's worth getting it right from the start. If you need to, work in a little flour, a tablespoon, or water, again, a tablespoon at a time, if the dough feels stiff or dry, or if you there are dry crumbs at the bottom of the bowl.

3. Tip out the dough onto a lightly floured worktop and **knead** it well for 10 minutes, or 4 minutes in a food-mixer using the dough hook attachment on the slowest speed. You want to make a very pliable, silky smooth dough; if it's sticking to your fingers or the worktop (or the sides of the mixer bowl) after kneading, work in a little more flour. The dough must be firm at this stage if the two layers are going to stick together later.
Continued

Try Something Different

To bump up the wow factor, add a tablespoon of poppy seeds to the flour along with the salt. Then at Step 6, brush the loaf with beaten egg and sprinkle with more poppy seeds. Score and bake the bread as per the method.

4. Put the dough back in the bowl, then cover the bowl tightly with clingfilm or a snap-on lid, or pop the bowl into a large plastic bag and close tightly. Leave to **rise** on the worktop for about 1½ hours at normal room temperature until doubled in size. Line the baking sheet with baking paper and sprinkle with flour.

5. Uncover the dough and punch it down (**knock back**) with your knuckles to deflate it, then turn it out onto a lightly floured worktop. Knead it gently for a minute to get rid of any large gas bubbles, then weigh it and cut off one-third. **Shape** both pieces of dough into neat balls, then roll them on the worktop using the palm of your hand until they are smooth and round. Put the balls on the prepared baking sheet spaced well apart to allow them to expand, then cover lightly with a sheet of clingfilm or slip the baking sheet into a large plastic bag and close tightly. Leave to **prove** and rise for 30–40 minutes at cool room temperature until almost doubled in size.

6. Towards the end of the rising time, preheat the oven to 230°C (210°C fan), 450°F, Gas 8 and put a roasting tin into the oven to heat up.

7. Uncover the risen balls of dough and gently flatten them with your fingers. Put the smaller ball on top of the larger one, wiggling it around until it is centred. Dip your fingers in flour, join two fingers and a thumb together to make a beak shape, and poke this into the middle of the loaf to press both pieces of dough together. Leave for 10 minutes, uncovered.

8. Very carefully brush all over with beaten egg glaze. Don't 'glue' the dough to the baking paper though.

9. Make vertical cuts round the edge of both dough balls with a sharp knife. Transfer the baking sheet to the oven, and quickly pour a jug of cold water or add ice cubes to the hot roasting tin to create a burst of steam (this helps develop a good **crust**). Close the door immediately. Bake for 15 minutes without opening the door. Reduce the oven temperature to 200°C (180°C fan), 400°F, Gas 6 and bake for another 20–25 minutes or until the loaf is a good golden brown (after 15 minutes, check to see that the loaf is browning evenly, if it isn't, turn the baking sheet). **Test** if the loaf is done by tapping it on the base; if it sounds hollow it is ready. Transfer to a wire rack to **cool**, then **store**. Eat within 4 days, but after that it is best toasted.

Onion Bread

This nutritious white and rye loaf is sweetened with a generous helping of slow-cooked, gently caramelised onion. Perfect to accompany hearty soups or creamy cheeses.

1 tablespoon extra virgin olive oil
1 large onion (about 150g), peeled, cut in half and sliced
sprig of fresh thyme
1 teaspoon balsamic vinegar or white wine
400g strong white bread flour, plus extra for dusting

100g stoneground wholegrain rye flour
8g fine sea salt
7g sachet fast-action dried yeast
about 325ml water, at room temperature

Easy does it

HANDS-ON TIME:
50 minutes

HANDS-OFF TIME:
2–2½ hours

BAKING TIME:
30–35 minutes

MAKES:
1 medium loaf

SPECIAL EQUIPMENT:
Baking sheet;
Roasting tin

STORAGE:
This is best eaten within 4 days

1. Heat the olive oil in a medium-sized heavy-based pan, add the onion and the sprig of thyme and stir well. Cut a disc of greaseproof or baking paper that is the circumference of your pan, run it under the cold tap to dampen it, then press the paper on top of the onion. Cover the pan tightly with the lid and reduce the heat so that the onion will cook very gently in its own steam until very tender, for about 30 minutes. Check and stir every 5 minutes or so.

2. Take off the lid and stir the onion gently over a medium–high heat until almost all the liquid has evaporated and the onion is just golden – don't let it burn. Stir the balsamic vinegar or white wine into the pan and dislodge all the bits of onion that are stuck on the bottom. Take the pan off the heat, leave the onions to cool, then pick out the thyme sprig. Line the baking sheet with baking paper.

3. Now start on the dough. Put the bread flour and the rye flour into a mixing bowl or the bowl of a food-mixer. Add the sea salt and **mix** it in using your hand or the dough hook attachment, then stir in the dried yeast and make a well in the centre.

4. Pour the water into the well and mix everything together to make a soft, slightly sticky dough – if it feels stiff or dry or there are dry crumbs at the bottom of the bowl, work in a little water, a tablespoon at a time; if it feels very sticky and clings to the sides of the bowl, work in a little flour. **Shape** the dough into a rough ball and leave it in the bowl, uncovered, for 5 minutes to allow the flours to absorb the water. After 5 minutes, prod the dough and work in a bit more water if it seems a bit stiff, but it will firm up as you knead it.
Continued

73

5. Turn out the dough onto a lightly floured worktop and **knead** it well for 10 minutes until firmer, very smooth and elastic (if you prefer, you can do this in a food-mixer using the dough hook for 5 minutes on the slowest speed). Spoon the cooled onion onto the dough.

6. Knead in the onion until it is evenly distributed; the dough will now feel quite sticky, but resist the temptation to add flour!

7. Put the dough back in the bowl and cover the bowl tightly with clingfilm or a snap-on lid, or pop it into a large plastic bag and close tightly. Leave on the worktop to **rise** for 1–1½ hours until doubled in size.

8. Uncover the dough and punch it down (**knock back**) with your knuckles to deflate it. Turn it out onto a lightly floured worktop and knead gently for 1 minute. Shape it into a ball, cover loosely with clingfilm and let it rest for 5 minutes.

9. Reshape the dough into a neat ball and put it on the prepared baking sheet. Slip the baking sheet into a large plastic bag or lightly cover the dough with clingfilm or a dry tea towel, and leave to **prove** and rise for about 1 hour until doubled in size.

10. Towards the end of the rising time, preheat the oven to 220°C (200°C fan), 425°F, Gas 7 and put a roasting tin in the bottom of the oven to heat up.

11. Cut three slashes in the top of the loaf with a very sharp knife, then put the baking sheet into the oven. Quickly pour a jug of cold water or add ice cubes to the hot roasting tin to create a burst of steam, then immediately close the door. This will help the loaf develop a good **crust**. Bake for 5 minutes, then reduce the oven temperature to 190°C (170°C fan), 375°F, Gas 5 and bake for a further 25–35 minutes until a good golden brown. **Test** the bread is done by tapping it on its base – if it sounds hollow it is cooked. Transfer to a wire rack and leave to **cool** then **store**. Best eaten within 4 days or toasted.

Breakfast Loaf

The perfect breakfast loaf for a nutritious boost to start the day. Soaking the seed mix for an hour before using stops the bread crumbling when sliced.

HANDS-ON TIME:
25 minutes

HANDS-OFF TIME:
3 hours

BAKING TIME:
30–35 minutes

MAKES:
1 large loaf

SPECIAL EQUIPMENT:
900g loaf tin (about 26 × 12.5 × 7.5cm)

STORAGE:
Once cold, wrap in clingfilm or pop into freezer bags and freeze for up to 1 month

50g wheatgerm with wheat bran
50g porridge oats
25g linseeds
25g sesame seeds
25g sunflower seeds
25g pumpkin seeds
10g fine sea salt
about 425ml lukewarm water

500g strong white bread flour, plus extra for dusting
7g sachet fast-action dried yeast
30g pine nuts
2 teaspoons soft-set honey

1. Grease the inside and the rim of the tin with butter. Put the wheatgerm/wheat bran mixture into a mixing bowl with the porridge oats, linseeds, sesame seeds, sunflower seeds, pumpkin seeds and the sea salt. Pour over 100ml of the lukewarm water and mix everything together well. Cover the bowl and leave the dry ingredients to soak for 1 hour.

2. Put the bread flour into a large mixing bowl or the bowl of a food-mixer, add the dried yeast and the pine nuts, and **mix** well with your hand or the dough hook attachment. Make a well in the centre, then add the soft-set honey. Pour in the remaining 325ml lukewarm water and work the dough so that it's just slightly firm but not dry or stiff. If the dough refuses to come together or there are dry crumbs at the bottom of the bowl, work in a little more lukewarm water a tablespoon at a time.

3. Turn out the dough onto a lightly floured worktop and **knead** well for 10 minutes, or put it in the food-mixer for 5 minutes with the dough hook on the slowest speed, until the dough feels much more pliable and elastic.

4. Tip the heavy, sticky, soaked mixture onto the dough and blend it in by kneading it gently for about 3 minutes until evenly distributed. The dough should feel heavy and slightly sticky, but don't be tempted to add more flour. Put the dough back in the bowl then cover the bowl tightly with clingfilm or a snap-on lid, or pop it into a large plastic bag and close tightly. Leave to **rise** on the worktop for about 1 hour at normal room temperature until doubled in size.

Continued

Try Something Different

If you prefer a deeper nutty taste and texture to this bread, leave out the pine nuts or replace them with chopped almonds or hazelnuts. For a touch of sweetness, add 25g dried cranberries with all the seeds in step 1.

5. Punch down (**knock back**) the risen dough to deflate it, then tip it out onto a lightly floured worktop. Dust your hands with flour and gently knead the dough for a minute, then **shape** it into a loaf that fits the tin. Flatten the dough with your fingers so it is a rectangular shape that's as wide as the tin is long and 2.5cm thick and start to roll it up, like a Swiss roll, from one short end.

6. Pinch the dough together each time you roll it until it is rolled up into a firm sausage shape, then pinch the seam firmly at the end.

7. With the seam-side underneath, tuck the ends under the roll and lift it into the prepared tin, seam-side down. Don't worry if there is space around the roll, as it will expand while it bakes. Slip the tin into a large plastic bag, letting in some air so that the plastic doesn't stick to the dough and close it tightly. Leave it to **prove** and rise at room temperature for about 1 hour until the loaf has almost doubled in size. Towards the end of that rising time, preheat the oven to 230°C (210°C fan), 450°F, Gas 8.

8. Uncover the loaf and cut some slashes down the centre of the top with a sharp knife. Bake for 15 minutes, then reduce the oven temperature to 200°C (180°C fan), 400°F, Gas 6 and bake for another 15–20 minutes until the loaf is a good golden brown. **Test** the bread is done by tapping the turned-out loaf on the base – it should sound hollow. Transfer to a wire rack and leave to **cool** before storing. Eat within 5 days or toasted.

Breadsticks

Made with a simple dough, breadsticks can be whipped up in no time. For something a little fancy, add some chopped olives, sesame seeds or grated cheese to the dough.

Easy does it

HANDS-ON TIME:
25 minutes

HANDS-OFF TIME:
1 hour 20 minutes

BAKING TIME:
12 minutes

MAKES:
16 breadsticks

SPECIAL EQUIPMENT:
1–2 baking sheets;
Pizza wheel-cutter

STORAGE:
Best eaten the same day or the next day

For the dough
300g strong white bread flour, plus extra for dusting
5g fine sea salt
7g sachet fast-action dried yeast
about 225ml lukewarm water
4 teaspoons olive oil, plus extra for greasing

To finish (optional)
125g pitted green and black olives, roughly chopped or 3 tablespoons sesame seeds or 2 tablespoons grated Parmesan

1. Line the baking sheet or sheets with baking paper. Put the bread flour and sea salt into a mixing bowl or the bowl of a food-mixer and combine with your hand or the dough hook attachment, then mix in the dried yeast.

2. Pour in the lukewarm water and **mix** it all together with your hand or the dough hook on the slowest speed. Feel the dough, it should be soft and sticky. Trickle in the olive oil, then **knead** again with your hand or the dough hook.

3. Lightly oil your fingers and the worktop, then turn out the dough and knead it well for 10 minutes, or for 5 minutes with the dough hook attachment on the slowest speed. The dough should feel a bit firmer, but very stretchy and soft. Now add flavour, if you like. Scatter the olives/sesame seeds/grated Parmesan over the dough and knead in gently with your hands to evenly distribute the chunks.

4. Put the dough back in the bowl and cover tightly with clingfilm or pop it into a large plastic bag and close tightly.

Leave to **rise** on the worktop for about 1 hour until doubled in size.

5. Dust your fingers and the worktop with flour then scrape out the dough without deflating it. Gently stretch and pat it into a rectangle, 16 × 34cm. Using a pizza wheel-cutter or large sharp knife, cut the dough into 16 × 16cm strips.

6. Pick up each strip, gently stretch and twist it, then put it on the lined baking sheet or sheets. Do this with all the strips, placing them a little apart. Don't worry if they untwist or look scruffy, it adds to their rustic charm. Cover loosely with clingfilm and leave on the worktop for 20 minutes to puff up.

7. Preheat the oven to 220°C (200°C fan), 425°F, Gas 7. Uncover the strips and bake for 12 minutes until golden – for crisp breadsticks, bake for another 4–5 minutes. Check them after 10 minutes and turn the sheet if they are not baking evenly. **Cool** them on a wire rack then eat them the same or the next day.

Pizzas and Pizzette

Little pizzas are perfect for feeding a crowd and you can have fun with toppings. The dough needs to be soft so that it can be stretched very thinly, so use minimal flour when kneading.

Easy does it

HANDS-ON TIME:
35 minutes

HANDS-OFF TIME:
1 hour or overnight

BAKING TIME:
8 minutes

MAKES:
4 individual pizzas or
25 pizzette

SPECIAL EQUIPMENT:
2–3 baking sheets or
pizza baking stone

STORAGE:
Best eaten the
same day

For the dough
500g strong white bread flour
7g fine sea salt
7g sachet fast-action dried yeast
1 tablespoon extra virgin olive oil, plus extra for greasing and kneading
about 300ml lukewarm water
cornmeal, for dusting

For the bianco topping
1 tablespoon green pesto
280g jar chargrilled artichokes in olive oil, drained and cut in half, 4 tablespoons oil reserved
175g log-style goats' cheese, cut into chunks

1. Put the bread flour and sea salt into a large mixing bowl or the bowl of a food-mixer and mix well with your hand or the dough hook attachment. Mix in the dried yeast and make a well in the centre.

2. Pour the olive oil and lukewarm water into the well and **mix** everything together with your hand or the dough hook on the slowest speed. You should get a soft but not sticky dough. If the dough feels stiff or dry or there are some stray dry crumbs at the bottom of the bowl, work in a little more lukewarm water, a tablespoon at a time; if the dough feels very sticky and clings to the sides of the bowl, work in a little flour.

3. Rub some oil over your hands and the worktop to stop the dough sticking, then turn out the dough and **knead** it really well for about 10 minutes, or 5 minutes using the dough hook on the slowest speed. It should feel very pliable, stretchy and silky smooth.
Continued

Try Something Different

• To make a margherita pizza, spread a thick tomato sauce over the pizza bases almost to the rim, as thinly as possible, then top with black olives and basil. Tear up mozzarella into rough chunks and divide equally among the bases and bake as above.
• For a caramelised onions and Gorgonzola topping, heat olive oil in a heavy-based pan, add 5 thinly sliced large red onions and a few fresh oregano leaves and cook, covered, on a very low heat for 35 minutes until very tender (stir occasionally). Uncover and stir over a medium–high heat until golden, then add a tablespoon white wine. Leave until cold, spread over the pizza bases almost to the rim, then top with 300g crumbled Gorgonzola piccante and bake as above.

4. Put the dough back in the bowl and cover the bowl tightly with clingfilm or a snap-on lid, or pop it into a large plastic bag and close tightly. Leave to **rise** on the worktop for about 1 hour until doubled in size, or if you want to make these in advance, you can leave it in the fridge overnight.

5. Meanwhile, make the bianco topping. Stir together the green pesto and artichoke oil in a small bowl.

6. Preheat the oven to its highest setting. If you are using a pizza baking stone, put this in the oven before you turn it on so it's nice and hot when you're ready to bake the pizza. Punch down (**knock back**) the risen dough with your knuckles to deflate it, then turn it out onto a lightly oiled worktop.

7. Weigh the dough and divide it into either 4 portions if you are making large pizzas, or 25 if you are making mini pizzas for a crowd. Lightly oil your hands then take the first ball of dough. If you are making 4 pizzas, pat, press and pull each portion of dough into a thin circle about 25cm across. Press your thumbs into the edges to make the dough slightly thicker and to make a 1.5cm rim all around. If you are making the mini pizza bases, roll the dough pieces into balls, then press them out with oiled fingers into a neat circle about 7.5cm across.

8. Cut some baking paper to fit your baking sheets and dust them with cornmeal. Arrange the pizza bases on the sheets.

9. Put the unlined baking sheets into the oven to heat up while you top your pizza bases. Give the pesto mixture a really good stir, then spread it thinly over the bases, almost to the rim.

10. Scatter over the artichokes and goats' cheese.

11. Take out the hot baking sheets, set them on a heatproof surface and carefully slide or lift the baking paper with the pizzas onto them. If you are using a pizza baking stone, carefully slide the paper onto the stone or, if you're feeling really confident, slide the pizza off the paper straight onto the stone.

12. Bake the larger pizzas for 8–10 minutes or until the edges are puffed, crisp and golden; bake the mini pizzas for 5–10 minutes, but keep an eye on them so they don't burn.

13. Eat the pizzas while still warm from the oven.

Gluten-free Loaf

There are a wide range of gluten-free and wheat-free flours and bread mixes available, but the finished result can often be disappointing. This bread is gluten-free and gorgeous.

400g all-purpose gluten-free baking flour
7g fine sea salt
2 teaspoons xanthan gum (check pack and omit if already in the flour mix)
1 tablespoon caster sugar
7g sachet fast-action dried yeast
1 medium egg, at room temperature
about 300ml lukewarm water
2 teaspoons low-fat plain yoghurt
1½ teaspoons rapeseed oil

Easy does it

HANDS-ON TIME:
10 minutes

HANDS-OFF TIME:
1–1½ hours

BAKING TIME:
30 minutes

MAKES:
1 small loaf

SPECIAL EQUIPMENT:
450g loaf tin (about 19 × 12.5 × 7.5cm)

STORAGE:
Once cold, wrap in clingfilm or pop into freezer bags and freeze for up to 1 month

1. Grease the inside and the rim of the tin with butter. Put the flour, sea salt, xanthan gum (if needed) and caster sugar into a large mixing bowl. Stir everything together with a wooden spoon, then stir in the dried yeast and make a well in the centre.

2. Break the egg into a measuring jug and add enough lukewarm water to make up the liquid to 350ml. Add the yoghurt and rapeseed oil to the egg mix and stir it really well with a fork. Pour this mixture into the well and **mix** it in for 2 minutes until it starts to make a very smooth, thick and sticky batter-like dough.

3. Scrape the dough into the prepared tin and spread it out evenly, pushing it into the corners. Slip the tin into a large plastic bag, letting in some air so that the plastic doesn't stick to the dough, and close it tightly. Leave to **rise** in a warm spot for 1–1½ hours until the dough has doubled in size.

4. Towards the end of the rising time, preheat the oven to 200°C (180°C fan), 400°F, Gas 6. Uncover the risen loaf and with a sharp knife score a neat diamond pattern over the top. Bake for 30–35 minutes until a good golden brown. **Test** the bread is done by tapping the base of the loaf – it should sound hollow. If there's a dull 'thud', put the loaf back in the oven on the shelf (you don't need to put it back in the tin) for another 5 minutes, then test again.

5. **Cool** the loaf on a wire rack and eat the same day or the by the next day.

Try Something Different

For a savoury version, pep it up with 2 tbsp chopped fresh chives or rosemary after adding the dried yeast.

Quick-cook
Flatbread Wraps

Perk up your lunch with these tasty little flatbreads. Roll them up with falafel and salad, hummus and olives, crumbled feta and tomatoes. For easy wrapping, roll the dough very thin.

Easy does it

HANDS-ON TIME:
20 minutes

HANDS-OFF TIME:
50–60 minutes

BAKING TIME:
2 minutes

MAKES:
4 flatbreads

SPECIAL
EQUIPMENT:
Griddle or large
heavy-based
frying pan

STORAGE:
Best eaten the same
day or the next day

50g stoneground wholemeal
bread flour
150g strong white bread flour, plus
extra for dusting
½ teaspoon fine sea salt
½ teaspoon fast-action dried yeast
(from a 7g sachet)
1 teaspoon olive oil
about 125ml lukewarm water

1. Put the wholemeal bread flour, white bread flour and the sea salt into a mixing bowl and **mix** well with your hand. Stir in the dried yeast and make a well in the centre.

2. Pour the olive oil and lukewarm water into the well and mix everything together with your hand to make a soft but not sticky dough. If the dough feels stiff or dry or there are stray dry crumbs at the bottom of the bowl, work in a little lukewarm water, a tablespoon at a time; if the dough feels sticky and clings to the sides of the bowl, work in a little flour.

3. Turn out the dough onto a very lightly floured worktop and **knead** well for 10 minutes until smooth and pliable. Put the dough back in the bowl, cover tightly with clingfilm and leave to **rise** in a warm spot for 50–60 minutes until doubled in size.

4. Turn out the dough onto a lightly floured worktop and gently knead it into a ball. Either divide the dough into 4 pieces by eye, or weigh it to be more precise. **Shape** each piece into a neat ball, then cover loosely with clingfilm or a clean, dry tea towel and leave to rest for 5 minutes.

5. With a lightly floured rolling pin, roll the balls into very thin 21cm circles.

6. Heat an ungreased griddle or heavy-based frying pan until very hot. Slide in a dough disc and cook for 1 minute. The disc will puff up, so flip the disc over and cook it for another minute, pressing down on the dough with a fish slice or metal spatula to get rid of the bubbles and so the dough on the underside comes into contact with the hot surface of the griddle/pan. Take it out of the pan and use immediately or leave to cool wrapped in a clean, dry tea towel. Cook the remaining breads in the same way.

7. Eat these the same or the next day – give them a quick blast under a hot grill.

Cheat's Sourdough

The cheat's sourdough; combining a small amount of yeast with part of the flour and 'pre-fermenting' it for 24 hours creates a chewy loaf with irregular holes and a great crust.

HANDS-ON TIME:
1 hour

HANDS-OFF TIME:
27–29½ hours

BAKING TIME:
30 minutes

MAKES:
2 medium loaves

SPECIAL
EQUIPMENT:
1–2 baking sheets;
Roasting tin

STORAGE:
Once cold, wrap
in clingfilm or pop
into freezer bags and
freeze for up to
1 month

50g either wholemeal rye flour or wholegrain spelt, or wheat bread flour or strong white bread flour
800g strong white bread flour, plus extra for dusting
1 teaspoon fast-action dried yeast (from a 7g sachet)
600ml room-temperature water
15g fine sea salt

1. Put the wholemeal rye/wholegrain spelt or wheat/strong white flour into a medium-sized mixing bowl with 300g of the white bread flour and dried yeast. **Mix** everything together with your hand, then pour in 350ml room-temperature water and mix well, still using your hand, to make a thick, sticky lump-free mixture.

2. Cover the bowl with a dampened tea towel and leave on the worktop, at normal room temperature, for 24 hours. Check the towel every few hours and dampen it if it gets a little dry.

3. The next day, uncover the bowl – the mixture should look bubbly and slightly greyer. Pour in the remaining 250ml room-temperature water and mix it in with your hand to make a smooth, runny batter. Pour this into a large bowl.
Continued

4. Tip half the remaining 500g flour into the batter and work it in with your hand, beating and stirring until fully incorporated. Mix in the 15g fine sea salt and gradually work in enough of the remaining 250g flour to make a soft but not sticky dough.

5. Lightly flour the worktop, then turn out the dough and **knead** it well for 10 minutes or until it feels very elastic. You can also do this in a large food-mixer using the dough hook on the slowest speed for 5 minutes.

6. Put the dough back in the bowl and cover the bowl tightly with clingfilm or a snap-on lid, or pop it into a large plastic bag and close tightly. Leave to **rise** on the worktop for about 3 hours until doubled in size. Check the dough after 2 hours, though, as it can take more or less time depending on how lively it is and the temperature of the room. Don't worry if it's not ready after 3 hours, just leave it and let it do its thing. When it starts to look ready, **line** the baking sheet or sheets with baking paper.

7. Punch down (**knock back**) the risen dough with your knuckles to deflate it, then turn it out onto a lightly floured worktop and cut it into two equal portions. Let these rest for 5 minutes, uncovered, then gently knead them for 1 minute each. **Shape** each piece into a neat ball and put them on the prepared baking sheet or sheets (if you can fit them onto 1 sheet, make sure they have plenty of space to expand while proving and baking).

8. Dust each ball of dough lightly with flour, then slip the baking sheet or sheets into a large plastic bag, letting in some air so the plastic doesn't stick to the dough and close it tightly, or cover loosely with clingfilm or a dry tea towel. Leave to **prove** and rise on the worktop for 1–1½ hours until doubled in size. Towards the end of the rising time, preheat the oven to 220°C (200°C fan), 425°F, Gas 7 and put a roasting tin in the bottom of the oven to heat up.

9. When the dough is ready for the oven, cut some slashes into the top of each loaf with a sharp knife, then put the sheet or sheets into the oven. Quickly pour a jug of cold water or add ice cubes to the hot roasting tin to create a burst of steam, then immediately close the door. This will help create a good **crust**. Bake for about 30 minutes until a good golden brown. To **test** if the loaves are done, tap them on the base with your knuckles: if they sound hollow, they are done; if there is a dull 'thud', put them back in the oven and bake for another 5 minutes, then test again. Leave the breads to **cool** on a wire rack before storing and eat within 5 days.

9

Naans

This dough is really quick and easy to prepare and when popped under a hot grill it puffs up until soft and fluffy. For a hotter flavour, add chopped chilli to the butter mix.

Easy does it

HANDS-ON TIME:
10 minutes

HANDS-OFF TIME:
1 hour

BAKING TIME:
3 minutes

MAKES:
8 medium or
4 large breads

SPECIAL
EQUIPMENT:
No kit needed, other
than a grill.

STORAGE:
Best eaten the
same day

250g self-raising flour, plus extra for dusting
½ teaspoon fine sea salt
½ teaspoon cracked black peppercorns or coarsely ground black pepper
or 1 teaspoon lightly toasted kalonji (black onion seeds or nigella)
or 1 teaspoon lightly toasted cumin seeds
3 rounded tablespoons plain live yoghurt (unsweetened)
115ml lukewarm water

To finish
50g unsalted butter
1–2 garlic cloves (to taste), peeled and crushed
2 tablespoons chopped fresh coriander

1. Put the self-raising flour, sea salt and cracked black peppercorns (or lightly toasted seeds) into a mixing bowl. **Mix** in the live yoghurt and lukewarm water, a little at a time, with your fingers until it makes a soft, slightly sticky and rough, shaggy-looking dough. Every flour is different, so you might need a bit more flour or water to get the perfect consistency. Work the dough in the bowl for a couple of seconds to make a ball.

2. Cover the bowl with clingfilm or a damp tea towel and leave in a warm spot for 1 hour to ferment. The dough won't rise as there is no yeast in it.

3. When ready to cook the naans, heat the grill and the wire grill rack until very hot.

4. Dust your fingers and the worktop with flour, then divide the dough into 8 equal portions. **Shape** each piece into a neat ball, then flatten and stretch each into a fairly thin oval about 18cm long.

5. Immediately cook the naans in batches under the grill for 1–1½ minutes on each side (you might need a little more or less time depending on your grill) until they puff up and are lightly speckled with brown spots.

6. While the naans cook, gently melt the butter with the crushed garlic cloves and stir in the chopped coriander.

7. As soon as the naans are cooked, takel them off the grill with kitchen tongs and brush them with the warm butter mixture. Eat immediately.

Pitta Breads

These ultra-thin pittas puff up when cooked, ready to be cut open and filled with falafel and salad. If you time how long the first one takes to cook, every pitta will be perfect.

450g strong white bread flour, plus extra for dusting
5g fine sea salt
7g sachet fast-action dried yeast
1 tablespoon extra virgin olive oil, plus extra for greasing
about 275ml lukewarm water

1. Put the bread flour and sea salt into a mixing bowl or the bowl of a food-mixer and **mix** well with your hand or the dough hook attachment. Stir in the dried yeast and make a well in the centre.

2. Pour the olive oil and lukewarm water into the well and gradually work the flour into the liquid with your hand or the dough hook on the slowest speed to make a soft but not sticky dough. If the dough feels stiff or dry or there are some stray dry crumbs at the bottom of the bowl, work in a little more lukewarm water, a tablespoon at a time; if the dough feels very sticky and clings to the sides of the bowl, work in a little flour.

3. Lightly rub your fingers and the worktop with a little olive oil, then turn out the dough and cover it with the upturned bowl; if you're using a food-mixer, cover the bowl with a snap-on lid or clingfilm. Leave to rest for 5 minutes.

4. Uncover the dough and **knead** it well for 10 minutes or 5 minutes with the dough hook attachment on the slowest speed.

5. Put the dough back into the bowl and cover the bowl tightly with clingfilm or a snap-on lid, or pop the bowl into a large plastic bag and close tightly. Leave to **rise** on the worktop for about 1 hour until doubled in size.
Continued

Try Something Different

To add a little flavour, gently knead in 2 tbsp chopped fresh coriander or chopped stoned olives at the end of the kneading time. If you prefer more robust breads, replace 50g of the white bread flour with wholemeal flour.

Easy does it

HANDS-ON TIME:
35 minutes

HANDS-OFF TIME:
1 hour 25 minutes

BAKING TIME:
3 minutes

MAKES:
12 pitta breads

SPECIAL EQUIPMENT:
Baking sheet or pizza baking stone

STORAGE:
Best eaten the same day or the next day

6. Lightly oil your fingers and the worktop again, then tip out the risen dough and punch it down (**knock back**) with your knuckles to deflate it. Weigh the dough and divide it into 12 equal portions. **Shape** each piece into a neat ball, then cover with clingfilm and leave to rest on the worktop for 10 minutes. This extra rest relaxes the dough so it is easier to shape. With a rolling pin, roll out each ball to a saucer-sized circle about 15cm across, or a slight oval shape, about 5mm thick.

7. Arrange the breads on a well-floured, clean, dry tea towel, cover lightly with clingfilm and leave to **prove** for 25 minutes until puffy.

8. While the pitta breads are proving and rising, preheat the oven to the highest temperature and heat the baking sheet or pizza baking stone in the oven.

9. When ready to bake, get a small bowl of water and put on some thick oven gloves. You will need to bake the pittas in batches, so open the oven and quickly put the pittas, 2 or 3 at a time, onto the very hot baking sheet or pizza baking stone, either with your gloved hands or with a long-handled ovenproof fish slice. Dip your fingers into the bowl of water and flick droplets over the breads, or you can 'mist' them with a water spray bottle just before baking. Don't do this while they are in the oven as you could damage it. Quickly close the door and leave them to bake for 2 minutes, then have a peek and make sure they are not colouring too much or unevenly. Turn the sheet if you think they are. Bake for another minute until they are lovely and puffy and lightly browned around the edges.

10. **Cool** the baked pittas on a wire rack and cover them with a dry tea towel to keep them soft. Eat warm or lightly grilled the same or next day.

Soft Sandwich Rolls

It's worth making a big batch of these soft white rolls because they freeze so well. Milk is the secret ingredient here, making a silky smooth dough and a delicious soft crumb.

650g strong white bread flour, plus extra for dusting
10g fine sea salt
2 teaspoons caster sugar
7g sachet fast-action dried yeast
50g unsalted butter, diced
about 400ml lukewarm milk
1 medium egg, at room temperature

To finish
extra milk, for brushing
sesame seeds, for sprinkling (optional)

1. **Line** the baking sheets with baking paper. Put the bread flour into a large mixing bowl or the bowl of a food-mixer with the sea salt and caster sugar and **mix** well with your hand or the dough hook attachment. Stir in the dried yeast and when everything is well mixed, rub in the butter with your fingertips until the mixture looks like fine crumbs. Then make a well in the centre.

2. Beat the lukewarm milk and the egg together with a fork, then pour this into the well. Mix everything together with your hand or using the dough hook on the slowest speed. If the dough feels stiff or dry or there are some stray dry crumbs at the bottom of the bowl, work in a little more lukewarm milk, a tablespoon at a time; if the dough feels very sticky and clings to the sides of the bowl, work in a little flour.

3. Dust your fingers and the worktop with flour and turn out the dough. **Knead** it well for 10 minutes or 5 minutes using the dough hook on the slowest speed until it feels firmer, silky-smooth and elastic. Put it back in the bowl and cover the bowl tightly with clingfilm or a snap-on lid, or pop it into a large plastic bag and close tightly. Leave to **rise** on the worktop for 1–1½ hours until doubled in size.
Continued

Try Something Different

If you are serving cocktail sausages as canape hot dogs you can make miniature bridge rolls. To make rolls with a sweet chilli flavour, add ¼ tsp dried chilli flakes when you add the sugar.

HANDS-ON TIME:
35 minutes

HANDS-OFF TIME:
1 ¾–2¼ hours

BAKING TIME:
10–20 minutes

MAKES:
18 finger rolls or burger buns, or 36 small bridge rolls

SPECIAL EQUIPMENT:
2 baking sheets

STORAGE:
Once cold, wrap in clingfilm or pop into freezer bags and freeze for up to 1 month

4. Punch down (**knock back**) the risen dough with your knuckles to deflate it, then turn it out onto a lightly floured worktop. Gently knead it for a minute until it feels very smooth and even. Now you need to weigh the dough. For large finger rolls and hamburger buns, divide the dough into 18 equal pieces (roughly 65g each); for small bridge rolls, divide the dough into 36 equal pieces.

5. For large finger rolls, shape the dough into neat balls and then roll them on the worktop with your hands to a neat sausage shape about 15cm long.

6. For hamburger buns, shape each portion of dough into a ball, then cup your hand over the ball so that your fingertips and wrist touch the work

surface and gently rotate your hand so the dough is rolled and smoothed into a neat, even ball. Gently flatten the ball to make a bun about 10cm across.

7. For small bridge rolls, shape each piece of dough into a neat oval by first rolling it into a ball, then into a cylinder the size of your little finger. Squeeze it gently between the sides of your hands to make a point at each end.

8. Arrange the rolls on the prepared baking sheets, spacing them a little apart to allow them to expand during baking, then slip each sheet into a large plastic bag, letting in some air so that the plastic doesn't stick to the dough and close tightly, or cover loosely with clingfilm. Leave to **prove** and rise as

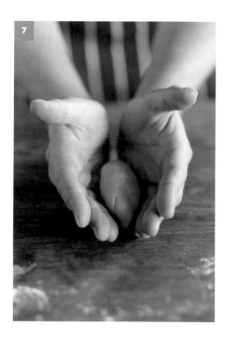

before for about 45 minutes until almost doubled in size. Towards the end of the rising time, preheat the oven to 230°C (210°Cfan), 450°F, Gas 8.

9. Uncover the dough and brush the buns lightly with milk, and if you like you can sprinkle over some sesame seeds. Bake for 5 minutes, then lower the oven temperature to 200°C (180°C fan), 400°F, Gas 6 and bake for another 5–10 minutes (depending on size and shape) until golden and firm.

10. Put the rolls and buns on a wire rack and cover immediately with a clean dry tea towel to keep the crusts soft. Eat within 24 hours.

Rosemary Potato Bread

A deliciously different loaf. Mashed potatoes and their cooking water add a wonderfully earthy flavour to this bread, which is studded with little chunks of olive oil-roasted potato.

375g floury or baking potatoes, scrubbed, 125g cut into 2cm chunks, 250g cut into bite-sized chunks
2 tablespoons olive oil
2 teaspoons roughly chopped rosemary
freshly ground black pepper
fine sea salt (2 pinches for sprinkling, 10g for the dough)
750g strong white bread flour, plus extra for dusting
7g sachet fast-action dried yeast

HANDS-ON TIME:
40 minutes

HANDS-OFF TIME:
1 ¾–2 hours

BAKING TIME:
30 minutes

MAKES:
2 medium loaves

SPECIAL EQUIPMENT:
1–2 baking sheets

STORAGE:
Best eaten the same day or the next day

1. Preheat the oven to 220°C (200°C fan), 425°F, Gas 7. Put the potatoes into an ovenproof dish with the olive oil and roast for 15 minutes until light gold and half cooked. As soon as the potatoes are ready, sprinkle over the chopped rosemary with a couple of grinds of black pepper and a couple of pinches of salt. Gently **mix** everything together and leave to cool. You can turn off the oven for now.

2. Put the remaining potato chunks into a pan with plenty of cold water to cover, then bring to the boil and cook for about 15 minutes until tender. Drain them, saving the cooking water in a heatproof jug or a pan. Put the drained potatoes back into the pan they were cooked in, cover with a tea towel and leave to dry for a couple of minutes. Mash the potatoes until nice and smooth and leave to cool.

3. To make the dough, put the bread flour into a large mixing bowl or the bowl of a food-mixer and add the sea salt. **Mix** well with your hand or the dough hook attachment, then stir in the dried yeast. Weigh out 175g of the cooled mashed potato (the rest you can keep for another recipe) and rub it into the flour with your fingers until all the lumps have gone.
Continued

Try Something Different

Lovage goes really well with potato; replace the rosemary with the same amount of this herb. For a loaf with a coarser, heartier texture, replace some or all the white flour with a wholemeal bread flour that has flecks of bran – you may need a little more water to bring the dough together.

4. Make a well in the mixture and pour in 400ml of the lukewarm potato water and stir it all together with your hand or the dough hook attachment on the slowest speed. It should come together as a fairly firm dough. If the dough feels stiff or dry or there are any dry crumbs left at the bottom of the bowl, drizzle in a little potato water or lukewarm tap water a tablespoon at a time; if the dough feels very sticky, work in a little flour.

5. Turn out the dough onto a lightly floured worktop and **knead** it well for 10 minutes or 4 minutes if you are using the dough hook on the slowest speed. It will become smooth and very elastic. Add the roast potatoes with the rosemary and olive oil and gently mix these through the dough by hand (don't use the dough hook or the chunks will break up) until evenly distributed. Put the dough back in the bowl and cover the bowl tightly with clingfilm or a snap-on lid. Leave to **rise** in a warm spot for about 1 hour until doubled in size. Line the baking sheet or sheets with baking paper.

6. Dust your fingers and the worktop with flour and gently press down the risen dough to deflate it. Turn it out onto the worktop and divide it in half – you can do this by eye but if you weigh it it will be more accurate. **Shape** each piece of dough into a circle about 20cm across and transfer to the prepared baking sheet or sheets – you might be able to fit both loaves on the same sheet, but remember to leave some space for them to expand.

7. Using a large sharp knife, deeply score each loaf into six wedges, cutting almost through the dough. Slip the sheet into a large plastic bag, letting in some air so that the plastic doesn't stick to the dough and close tightly, or cover loosely with clingfilm. Leave to **prove** and rise for 45–60 minutes until doubled in size.

8. Towards the end of the proving time, preheat the oven to 220°C (200°C fan), 425°F, Gas 7. Uncover the dough and bake the loaves for about 30 minutes until they are a good golden brown. Check them after 25 minutes though, and if they look like they are not browning evenly, turn the sheet or sheets. To **test** the bread is cooked tap it on the base – it should sound hollow. Leave to **cool** a little on a wire rack and eat warm the same day or the next day.

Olive and Rosemary Focaccia

Focaccia is a rustic Italian flatbread which is simply flavoured with olive oil, herbs and crunchy salt. Its light, open texture is created by thoroughly kneading a fairly soft dough.

500g strong white bread flour
8g fine sea salt
1 tablespoon fresh rosemary leaves
7g sachet fast-action dried yeast
3 tablespoons extra virgin olive oil, plus extra for greasing
about 300ml lukewarm water
85g small whole stoned black olives, roughly chopped

To finish
a few sprigs fresh rosemary
about 3 tablespoons extra virgin olive oil

Easy does it

HANDS-ON TIME:
25 minutes

HANDS-OFF TIME:
2¼–3¼ hours

BAKING TIME:
20–25 minutes

MAKES:
1 large loaf

SPECIAL EQUIPMENT:
Roasting tin, cake tin or baking tin (about 22 × 30cm)

STORAGE:
Best eaten on the same day

1. Put the bread flour into a mixing bowl or the bowl of a food-mixer and stir in the sea salt. Chop the rosemary leaves as finely or as roughly as you like and stir in the dried yeast using your hand or the dough hook attachment. Make a well in the centre.

2. Pour the olive oil into the well, followed by the lukewarm water and **mix** everything together with your hand or the dough hook attachment on the slowest speed. The dough should be lovely and soft and slightly sticky. If there are dry crumbs at the bottom of the bowl or the dough feels stiff or dry, work in a little more lukewarm water, a tablespoon at a time; if the dough feels very sticky and clings to the sides of the bowl, work in a little more flour.

3. Rub a little olive oil onto your fingers and the worktop (but you don't want an oil slick!), then turn out the dough and **knead** it well for 10 minutes or 5 minutes with the dough hook on the slowest speed. The dough should feel slightly firmer and very pliable and stretchy. Gently work the chopped olives into the dough. Put the dough back in the bowl and cover the bowl tightly with clingfilm or a snap-on lid, or pop it into a large plastic bag and close tightly. Leave to **rise** on the worktop for 1–1½ hours at normal room temperature until doubled in size. Grease the tin with olive oil.

Continued

4. Oil your fingers and the worktop again, then gently turn out the dough without deflating it. Gently press and pull the dough between your hands into a rectangle that will fit your tin, then press it into the prepared tin, getting the dough right into the corners. Try to have a really light touch with the dough, don't handle it too much or try to get it neat and tidy, we're going for a rustic look and a lovely open texture. Slip the tin into a large plastic bag, letting in some air so that the plastic doesn't stick to the dough and close tightly, or cover with a damp tea towel. Leave the dough in a warm or sunny spot to rise for 45–60 minutes until almost but not quite doubled in size.

5. To finish, pull the remaining rosemary into tiny sprigs of 2 or 3 leaves. Uncover the dough, then push little dimples about 1cm deep into the dough by prodding it firmly with your fingertips.

6. Tuck the rosemary into the indentations at regular intervals. Cover as before and leave to **prove** and rise for 30–45 minutes until the dough has doubled in size.

7. Towards the end of the proving time, preheat the oven to 220°C (200°C fan), 425°F, Gas 7. Uncover the dough and dribble about 3 tablespoons extra virgin olive oil over it so that there are little puddles of oil in the dimples. Don't overdo it, though, as too much oil will make the finished bread soggy and damp.

8. Bake for 20–25 minutes until the loaf is a good golden brown.

9. The focaccia needs to be turned out of the tin or the oil will make it go soggy, so do this carefully to avoid burning yourself with the hot oil. Eat it while still warm – it doesn't keep or freeze well.

Wild Mushroom and Thyme Spelt Fougasse

This French loaf is made for tearing and sharing, preferably while warm from the oven, dipped in olive oil and balsamic vinegar. Shaping the dough will challenge your creative side.

10g dried porcini mushrooms or dried wild mushroom pieces, large pieces torn
200ml boiling water
275g white spelt flour suitable for breadmaking, plus extra for dusting
75g stoneground wholegrain spelt flour
5g fine sea salt

7g sachet fast-action dried yeast
1 teaspoon fresh thyme leaves

To finish
fresh thyme leaves

1. Tip the dried porcini mushrooms or dried wild mushroom pieces into a heatproof bowl and pour over the boiling water. Leave to hydrate until the water has cooled to lukewarm.

2. Put the white and wholegrain spelt flours into a mixing bowl or the bowl of the food-mixer with the sea salt and **mix** in with your hand or the dough hook attachment. Stir in the yeast and thyme and make a well in the centre.

3. Set a small sieve over a measuring jug and drain the mushrooms into it. Press down on the mushrooms to squeeze out as much liquid as possible, then scoop out the mushrooms into the flour well. Add enough lukewarm water to the mushroom liquid to bring it up to 225ml and pour it into the well. Give everything a good stir with your hand or the dough hook on the slowest speed. You should get a soft but not sticky dough. If there are dry crumbs lurking at the bottom of the bowl or the dough feels stiff or dry, work in more lukewarm water, a tablespoon at a time.

4. Lightly dust your hands and the worktop with flour, then turn out the dough onto the worktop. Cover the dough with the upturned bowl (or cover the mixer bowl with a tea towel or snap-on lid) and let it rest for 5 minutes. Uncover the dough and start to **knead** it – if it feels a bit stiff or dry, work in a little more lukewarm water. Knead the dough well for 10 minutes or 5 minutes with the dough hook on the slowest speed. It should feel very stretchy and pliable. Cover the dough with the upturned bowl or loosely cover with a sheet of clingfilm and leave to rest for 15 minutes. This will make the dough easier to shape.
Continued

Try Something Different

For a herb-flavoured green and black olive bread, leave out the dried mushrooms and make the dough with 225ml lukewarm water. At the end of kneading, mix in 150g pitted green and black olives flavoured with herbs, then finish the recipe as below.

5. Cut a sheet of baking paper to fit your baking sheet and set it on the worktop. Flour your fingers again and then pat out the dough into an oval about 25 × 20cm. Carefully lift it onto the baking paper and tweak the shape if you need to. Cover loosely with a dry tea towel or clingfilm and leave to **rise** for about I hour until almost doubled in size.

6. Towards the end of the rising time, preheat the oven to 230°C (210°C fan), 450°F, Gas 8. Put the baking sheet in the oven to heat up and a roasting tin in the bottom of the oven. Uncover the dough and scatter with fresh thyme leaves.

7. Using a small, sharp knife, cut 5 slits, about 10cm long, in the dough, a bit like veins in a leaf.

8. Flour your fingers and gently prise open the slits to make large lozenge-shaped holes about 6cm wide.

9. Carefully remove the hot baking sheet from the oven, place it on a heatproof surface, lift the loaf on its sheet of baking paper onto it and put it in the oven. Quickly pour a jug of cold water or add ice cubes to the hot roasting tin to create a burst of steam, then immediately close the door. This will help create a good **crust**. Bake for

12–15 minutes until the bread is a good golden brown and sounds hollow when tapped on the base. Put on a wire rack and for a couple of minutes, but eat it while still warm.

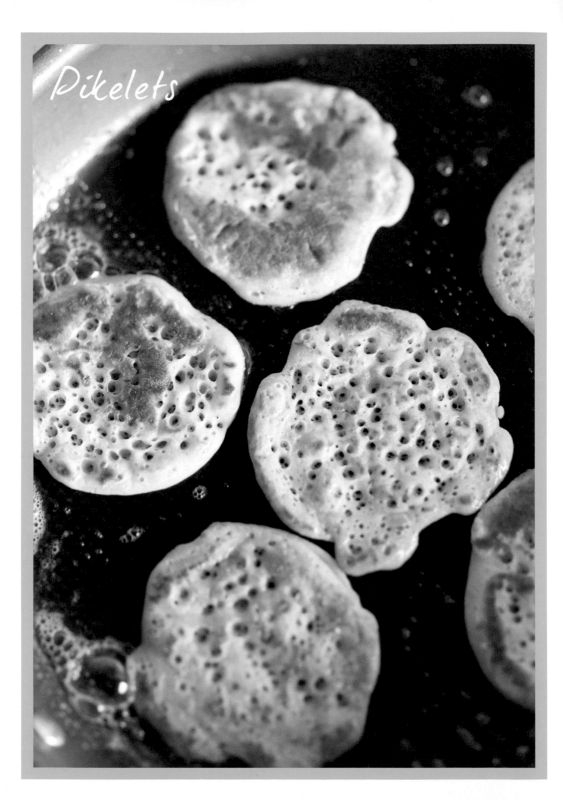

Pikelets

Cups of steaming tea are perfectly complemented by hot pikelets with butter melting through their holes. An informal version of a crumpet, pikelets have a crisp base and light texture.

115g strong white bread flour
115g plain white flour
½ teaspoon cream of tartar
1 teaspoon fast-action dried yeast (from a 7g sachet)
250ml lukewarm water
½ teaspoon fine sea salt
¼ teaspoon bicarbonate of soda
140ml lukewarm milk

1. Sift the bread flour, plain flour and cream of tartar into a mixing bowl. Stir in the dried yeast with your hand.

2. Pour in the lukewarm water and **mix** into the flour with your hand, then continue to beat the mixture for 2 minutes to make a smooth, thick batter. Cover the bowl tightly with clingfilm and leave in a warm spot for 1 hour – the batter will **rise** up and then flop back down again – that's normal!

3. Uncover the bowl, sprinkle the sea salt over the batter and beat well with your hand for a minute. Cover the bowl again and leave for 20 minutes.

4. Stir the bicarbonate of soda into the lukewarm milk, then gently stir it into the batter with a wooden spoon until well combined – it should be a thick, smooth, pourable batter.

5. Heat the ungreased griddle or heavy-based frying pan until very hot. Stir the batter, then drop 2 tablespoons onto the griddle/pan so it makes a rough circle about 9–10cm across. Cook for 3 minutes until the top is peppered with with holes and the underside is golden brown, then flip the pikelet over with a palette knife or metal spatula and carry on cooking for another 2–3 minutes until the holey side is speckled brown. You may need to adjust the heat, as the pan needs to be hot or the pikelets will be tough and soggy. Cook the remaining mixture in batches and eat the pikelets straight from the griddle, smothered with butter, or leave them to cool, wrapped in a clean dry tea towel, and then toast them.

Try something different

For cheese pikelets, stir in 100g finely grated mature Cheddar and a good pinch of cayenne pepper after adding the milk.

Needs a little skill

HANDS-ON TIME:
15 minutes

HANDS-OFF TIME:
1 hour 20 minutes

BAKING TIME:
5–6 minutes

MAKES:
18

SPECIAL EQUIPMENT:
Griddle or heavy-based frying pan

STORAGE:
Once cold, wrap in clingfilm or pop into freezer bags and freeze for up to 1 month. They can be toasted from frozen

117

Swirled Chorizo
Bread

The perfect Mediterranean picnic loaf, this dough has a firm consistency so holds its shape when rolled up and baked. You can also cut it into slices for pinwheel breads (see below).

Needs a
little skill

500g strong white bread flour
8g fine sea salt
7g sachet fast-action dried yeast
3 tablespoons extra virgin olive oil,
plus extra for greasing/brushing
about 275ml lukewarm water
fine cornmeal or polenta, for dusting

To finish
100g chorizo, skinned and finely diced
75g sundried tomatoes in oil, drained
and cut into thin strips
about 3 tablespoons extra virgin olive
oil, for brushing

HANDS-ON TIME:
25 minutes

HANDS-OFF TIME:
1¾–2½ hours

BAKING TIME:
35 minutes

MAKES:
1 large loaf or 16
individual breads

**SPECIAL
EQUIPMENT:**
900g loaf tin (about
26 × 12.5 × 7.5cm)

STORAGE:
Best eaten the same
day or the next day

1. Put the bread flour into a mixing bowl or the bowl of a food-mixer and stir in the sea salt. **Mix** in the dried yeast using your hand or the dough hook attachment. Make a well in the centre.

2. Pour the olive oil into the well, followed by the lukewarm water and mix everything together with your hand or the dough hook attachment on the slowest speed to make a very soft dough. If there are dry crumbs at the bottom of the bowl or the dough feels stiff or dry, work in more lukewarm water a tablespoon at a time; if the dough feels very sticky and clings to the sides of the bowl, work in a little more flour.

3. Rub a little olive oil onto your fingers and the worktop (you don't want an oil slick!), then turn out the dough and **knead** thoroughly for 10 minutes or 5 minutes with the dough hook on the slowest speed, or until the dough feels slightly firmer and elastic. Return the dough to the bowl, if necessary, then cover the bowl tightly with clingfilm or a snap-on lid, or slip it into a large plastic bag and close tightly. Leave to

rise on the worktop for 1–1½ hours at normal room temperature until doubled in size. Grease the inside and the rim of the tin with olive oil.

Continued

Try Something Different

For individual pinwheel breads, make the dough up to the end of Step 4. Using a sharp knife, cut the roll into 16 even slices. Arrange, cut-side up and well apart on a baking sheet lined with baking paper. Leave to prove as in Step 6, brush the cut surface of each swirl lightly with olive oil, then bake for 15–20 minutes until a good golden brown. Transfer to a wire rack and brush lightly with olive oil again, then drizzle with balsamic glaze and eat while warm. For a less spicy flavour, replace the chorizo and sundried tomatoes with 100g tapenade and 50g toasted pine nuts.

4. Sprinkle a little fine cornmeal or polenta onto the worktop, then turn out the dough and press it out with your fingers into a rectangle about 24 × 28cm. Scatter over the chorizo, then the sundried tomatoes.

5. Start to roll up the dough like a Swiss roll starting from one short side.

6. Keep rolling, pinching the seam together firmly each time you roll the dough over. Don't skip this step or the baked loaf may have gaps in the swirl.

7. When you have finished rolling, pinch the final seam to seal firmly. Tuck the ends under the roll and lift the dough into the prepared tin, seam-side down.

8. Slip the tin into a large plastic bag, letting in some air so that the plastic doesn't stick to the dough and close tightly, or cover with a damp tea towel and leave to **prove** in a warm or sunny spot for 45–60 minutes until almost but not quite doubled in size. Towards the end of the proving time, preheat the oven to 220°C (200°C fan), 425°F, Gas 7. Uncover the risen dough and lightly brush the dough with olive oil.

9. Bake the loaf for about 35 minutes until it is a good golden brown. To **test** if the bread is cooked, tap the loaf on the base – it should sound hollow.

10. Carefully turn out onto a wire rack and leave to **cool** before slicing. Best eaten the same or next day, or lightly grilled.

Stuffed Focaccia

This soft and silky focaccia 'sandwich' is a meal in itself. Stuff it full of your favourite fresh Mediterranean ingredients and flavours, but seal the dough well so they don't escape!

Needs a little skill

HANDS-ON TIME:
25 minutes

HANDS-OFF TIME:
1 hour 45 minutes

BAKING TIME:
25–30 minutes

MAKES:
1 large filled bread

SPECIAL EQUIPMENT:
Roasting tin or baking tin (not loose-based) about 20 × 30cm; Dough scraper

STORAGE:
Best eaten on the same day

For the dough
500g strong white bread flour
7g fine sea salt
1 teaspoon fresh thyme leaves
7g sachet fast-action dried yeast
3 tablespoons virgin olive oil, plus extra for greasing/brushing
about 325ml lukewarm water

For the filling
100g prosciutto
280g jar roasted or chargrilled mixed peppers in olive oil, well drained
¼ teaspoon dried red chilli flakes, or to taste
100g pecorino cheese, rind removed and thinly sliced

1. First make the dough. Mix the bread flour and the sea salt in a large mixing bowl or the bowl of a food-mixer with your hand or the dough hook attachment. Sprinkle in the thyme leaves and the dried yeast and **mix** them in well. Then make a well in the centre.

2. Pour the olive oil and lukewarm water into the well and mix everything together with your hand or the dough hook on the slowest speed to make a very soft, slightly sticky dough. If there are dry crumbs at the bottom of the bowl or the dough feels stiff or dry, work in a little more lukewarm water, a tablespoon at a time.

3. Rub a little olive oil onto your fingers and the worktop, just enough to prevent the dough sticking, and turn out the dough. **Knead** it well for 10 minutes or 5 minutes using the dough hook on the slowest speed until it is firmer and, this is the important bit, very elastic and stretchy. Put the dough back in the bowl and cover the bowl tightly with clingfilm or a snap-on

lid, or pop it into a large plastic bag and close tightly. Leave to **rise** on the worktop for about 1 hour at normal room temperature until doubled in size. Grease the tin with olive oil.
Continued

Try Something Different

You can easily adapt this recipe to include your favourite combinations of Mediterranean ingredients, use thinly sliced salami or pepperoni instead of the prosciutto, or 75g fresh young spinach leaves; replace the peppers with chargrilled sun-dried tomatoes (from a 280g jar in olive oil) or scatter with stoned olives; or swap the strong pecorino cheese for a milder crumbled goats' cheese, slices of firm mozzarella or some thin shavings of Parmesan.

4. Uncover the risen dough, oil your fingers and worktop again, and turn out the dough. Don't punch it down, just cut the ball into two equal pieces using an oiled dough scraper or a large knife. Lightly cover one portion with clingfilm, then press, pat and stretch out the other piece of dough into a rectangle that will fit your tin. Lift the dough into the tin and gently push it out into the sides – it will spring back, but play the game and keep pushing it back until the dough finally gives in and is of an even thickness and fits the tin. Arrange the 100g prosciutto in an even layer over the dough, but leave a 1cm dough border all around.

5. Dot the 280g drained roasted or chargrilled mixed peppers evenly over the prosciutto, then sprinkle with the ¼ teaspoon dried red chilli flakes. Finish with a layer of the 100g thinly sliced pecorino cheese.

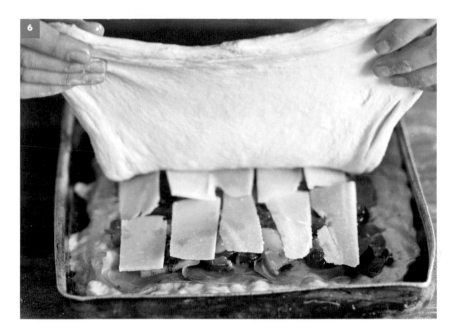

6. Press and pat out the second piece of dough to a rectangle that fits the tin, and lay it over the filling as a lid. Oil your fingers and gently stretch and pat the dough in place so that it completely covers the filling. Gently push out any air pockets in the dough then pinch the two layers together right round the edge to seal in the filling. Make a few air holes in the top layer of dough with the tip of a small knife. Slip the tin into a large plastic bag, letting in a bit of air so that the plastic doesn't stick to the dough, and close tightly. Leave to **prove** and rise at normal room temperature for about 45 minutes until almost doubled in size.

7. Towards the end of the rising time, preheat the oven to 220°C (200°C fan), 425°F, Gas 7. Uncover the tin and lightly brush the top of the focaccia with olive oil. Bake for 25–30 minutes or until crisp and golden brown. Carefully turn out onto a wire rack and leave to **cool** – if it cools in the tin you will lose that lovely crispness as the base of the focaccia will go soggy as the steam condenses. Cut into large squares and eat warm from the oven or at room temperature on the same day.

Pretzels

Soft and chewy pretzels are easy to make but moulding the dough will call upon your creative shaping skills. Don't fret, though, they don't need to be perfect – they suit a rustic look!

Needs a little skill

300g strong white bread flour, plus extra for dusting
5g caster sugar
5g fine sea salt
7g sachet fast-action dried yeast
about 225ml lukewarm milk

To finish
1 egg plus a pinch of salt, for glazing
sea salt flakes, for sprinkling
or 3 tablespoons sesame seeds
or 3 tablespoons grated mature Cheddar
30g unsalted butter

HANDS-ON TIME:
35 minutes

HANDS-OFF TIME:
45 minutes

BAKING TIME:
15–20 minutes

MAKES:
8 pretzels

SPECIAL EQUIPMENT:
2 baking sheets

STORAGE:
Best eaten on the same day

1. Put the bread flour, caster sugar and sea salt into a large mixing bowl or the bowl of a food-mixer and **mix** well with your hand or the dough hook attachment. Stir in the dried yeast and make a well in the centre.

2. Pour the lukewarm milk into the well and mix everything together with your hand or the dough hook attachment on the slowest speed. It should make a fairly soft but not sticky dough. If there are dry crumbs at the bottom of the bowl or the dough feels stiff or dry, work in more lukewarm milk a tablespoon at a time. Leave the dough uncovered in the bowl for 5 minutes for the flour to hydrate – after this, if the dough feels firm rather than soft, work in a little more milk.

3. Dust your hands and the worktop with flour and turn out the dough. **Knead** it well for about 10 minutes by hand or 5 minutes with the dough hook on the slowest speed until it feels firmer, very pliable and elastic. Put the dough back in the bowl and cover the bowl tightly with clingfilm or a snap-on lid, or pop it into a large plastic bag and close tightly. Leave on the worktop to **rise** for 30 minutes until the dough looks puffy.

4. Punch down (**knock back**) the dough with your knuckles to deflate it, then turn it out onto an unfloured worktop. The slight friction will help you shape the dough rather than it sliding around. Weigh the dough and divide it into 8 equal portions. **Shape** each piece into a rough ball, then leave uncovered on the worktop to rest for 5 minutes. Line the baking sheets with baking paper.
Continued

5. Now it's time to get arty and shape the pretzels. Roll each ball of dough, using your hands, into a thin, even sausage about 46cm long – if the dough starts to stick to your fingers, just dust them lightly with flour.

6. Shape a sausage into a wide U, then lift one end and set it on top of the base of the U on the opposite side.

7. Do the same with the other end – the bent 'legs' of the U should now be crossing in the middle of the shape.

8. If you're feeling confident, you can make a more fancy shape by rolling the sausage to 50cm long, then twisting the two 'legs' as they cross in the middle.

9. Carefully lift the shaped pretzels onto the prepared baking sheets, trying not to undo all your artistry, and place them well apart to give them room to expand. Leave uncovered on the worktop for 15 minutes.

10. Meanwhile, preheat the oven to 220°C (200°C fan), 425°F, Gas 7. Using a fork, beat the 1 medium egg with a pinch of salt and 1 tablespoon cold water to make the glaze, then very lightly brush it over the pretzels. Be careful not to 'glue' the dough to the baking paper. Sprinkle over some sea salt flakes, the 3 tablespoons sesame seeds or grated mature Cheddar, then bake for 15–20 minutes until golden brown. Take a peek after 10 minutes and if the pretzels aren't browning evenly, turn the sheet.

11. Towards the end of the baking time, melt the 30g unsalted butter and as soon as the pretzels are ready, take the baking sheets out of the oven, set them on a heatproof surface and quickly brush the pretzels with the melted butter. Put the pretzels onto a wire rack lined with fresh baking paper and leave to **cool** slightly. They are best eaten still warm from the oven or the same day.

Bagels

Bagels are a favourite food on the go. Their glossy, chewy crust hides a soft, spongy textured crumb, created by quickly poaching the dough rings in malted boiling water before baking.

500g extra-strong white bread flour, plus extra for dusting
8g fine sea salt
20g caster sugar
7g sachet fast-action dried yeast
250ml lukewarm water
1 medium egg, at room temperature
2 teaspoons malt extract
2 tablespoons sunflower oil or melted butter

To finish
1 tablespoon malt extract, for poaching
1 egg white plus a pinch of salt, for glazing
sesame seeds, poppy seeds, sunflower seeds, black onion (nigella) seeds or caraway seeds, for sprinkling (your choice or optional)

HANDS-ON TIME:
50 minutes

HANDS-OFF TIME:
1¾ hours

BAKING TIME:
20–25 minutes

MAKES:
12 bagels

SPECIAL EQUIPMENT:
3 baking sheets

STORAGE:
Once cold, wrap in clingfilm or pop into freezer bags and freeze for up to 1 month.

1. Put the white bread flour, sea salt and caster sugar into a large mixing bowl or the bowl of a food-mixer and **mix** well with your hand or the dough hook attachment. Stir in the dried yeast and make a well in the centre.

2. Pour the lukewarm water into the measuring jug, then break the egg into it, add the malt extract and sunflower oil or melted butter and beat everything together with a fork until combined. Pour this liquid into the well in the flour, then with your hand or the dough hook on the slowest speed, gradually tip the flour into the liquid and mix it in to make a soft but not sticky dough. If there are dry crumbs at the bottom of the bowl or the dough feels stiff or dry, work in more lukewarm milk a tablespoon at a time. Cover the bowl with clingfilm, a snap-on lid or a damp tea towel and leave it to rest for 10 minutes – this will make kneading the dough easier.

3. Turn out the dough onto a lightly floured worktop and **knead** very thoroughly for 10 minutes or 5 minutes using the dough hook on its slowest speed until the dough feels very elastic and smooth.

4. Return the dough to the bowl, if necessary, then cover the bowl tightly with clingfilm or a snap-on lid, or pop it into a large plastic bag and close tightly. Leave to **rise** on the worktop for about 1½ hours at normal room temperature until doubled in size.

5. Punch down (**knock back**) the risen dough with your knuckles to deflate it, then turn it out onto a lightly floured work surface. **Shape** it into a ball – just roughly, it doesn't need be perfect – then weigh it and divide it into 12 equal portions. Shape each into a neat ball, then cover with a dry tea towel and leave to rest for 10 minutes, to help make shaping the dough easier.
Continued

6. Slightly flatten the balls with your hands, then push a floured forefinger through the centre of each ball, one at a time, to make a sort of doughnut ring. Gently twirl the ring on your finger to stretch the dough and make the hole bigger. It will close up a bit as it cooks, so try to make the hole about 3cm across to start with.

7. Put the bagels on a well-floured baking sheet, spacing them well apart, cover them again with the dry tea towel and leave for 15 minutes. Line the two other baking sheets with baking paper.

8. Meanwhile, heat the oven to 200°C (180°C fan), 400°F, Gas 6.

9. Bring a large saucepan of water to the boil and stir in the 1 tablespoon malt extract (this will give the bagels that lovely shiny golden crust). Gently drop the bagels, 2 or 3 at a time (not too many as they swell as they cook) into the boiling water and poach for exactly 30 seconds. Using a slotted spoon, carefully flip them over and poach for another 30 seconds.

10. Lift out the bagels with the slotted spoon, draining them thoroughly, and put them on the lined baking sheets, spacing them well apart.

11. When all the bagels have been poached, beat the 1 egg white with a pinch of salt just until broken up, then very lightly brush it over the bagels to glaze. Don't get the glaze on the baking paper as this will 'glue' the dough to it.

12. Leave the bagels plain or you can sprinkle them with the seeds, then bake them for 20–25 minutes until they are a glossy golden brown. Remove from the oven and put them on a wire rack to **cool** completely. Best eaten the same or next day, or toasted.

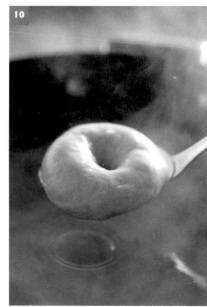

Deep Dark Rye Bread

If the dense texture of rye bread doesn't appeal, this will change your mind. As in the Cheat's Sourdough (see page 90), a poolish gives this loaf a soft, open crumb and rich flavour.

For the poolish
250g stoneground wholegrain rye flour, plus extra for dusting
1 teaspoon fast-action dried yeast (from a 7g sachet)
300ml lukewarm water

To finish the dough
200g stoneground wholegrain rye flour
100g strong white bread flour
8g fine sea salt
1 teaspoon caraway seeds
125ml lukewarm water

To finish
milk, for brushing
caraway seeds or rye flakes, for sprinkling

Needs a little skill

HANDS-ON TIME:
40 minutes

HANDS-OFF TIME:
7 hours

BAKING TIME:
35–40 minutes

MAKES:
2 medium loaves

SPECIAL EQUIPMENT:
Baking sheet;
Roasting tin

STORAGE:
Once cold, wrap in clingfilm or pop into freezer bags and freeze for up to 1 month

1. Start by making the poolish. Put the wholegrain rye flour and dried yeast into a mixing bowl, **mix** well with your hand, then pour in the lukewarm water and mix to make a smooth, thick batter. Cover the bowl with clingfilm and leave on the worktop to **rise** for 4 hours.

2. When you are ready to finish the dough, mix the wholegrain rye flour, the white bread flour and the sea salt in a separate mixing bowl or the bowl of a food-mixer. Pour in the lukewarm water and stir the poolish (from Step 1). Mix everything together with your hand or with the dough hook attachment on the slowest speed. You should get a very soft and sticky, heavy dough. Leave it in the bowl for 5 minutes, uncovered, so that the flour can fully hydrate. If it feels a bit stiff after that, work in a little more lukewarm water, a tablespoon at a time.

3. Turn out the dough onto a very lightly floured worktop and **knead** it well for 10–12 minutes or 5–6 minutes with the dough hook on the slowest speed. The dough should feel slightly firmer but pliable; don't worry if it feels rather heavy and sticky, that's fine, it's different to an all-white bread dough. *Continued*

Try Something Different

For extra flavour, add another teaspoon of caraway seeds and a couple of good pinches of ground coriander; or omit the seeds and add 2 tbsp raisins to the flours with the salt.

4. Put the dough back in the bowl and cover the bowl tightly with clingfilm or a snap-on lid, or pop it into a large plastic bag and close tightly. Leave in a warm but not hot place to rest and **rise** for I hour.

5. Punch down (**knock back**) the dough with your knuckles – it will feel quite lively – roll it into a ball, then cover and leave as before for I hour.

6. Turn out the dough onto a lightly floured worktop, knead it a couple of times, then divide it into two equal portions. **Shape** each piece into a ball, cover loosely with clingfilm or a dry tea towel and leave to rest for I0 minutes. Line the baking sheet with baking paper.

7. Knead and shape each ball of dough into an oval loaf about 20cm long, make a deep crease down the length of the oval with the side of your hand, then fold the dough over. Now roll the dough over on the worktop so that the join is underneath and the loaf is a neat oval shape. Put the loaf onto the prepared baking sheet with the join underneath, keeping the shape intact. Shape the second piece of dough in the same way and put it on the baking sheet, well away from the first loaf so they have room to expand. Slip the baking sheet into a large plastic bag, letting in some air so that the plastic doesn't stick to the dough and close tightly. Leave to **prove** and rise for about I hour until nearly doubled in size.

8. Towards the end of the rising time, preheat the oven to 220°C (200°C fan), 425°F, Gas 7 and put a roasting tin in the bottom of the oven to heat up.

9. Uncover the loaves and brush lightly with a little milk, then sprinkle with caraway seeds or rye flakes.

10. Slash the top of each loaf three times, using a very sharp knife, then put them into the oven. Quickly pour a jug of cold water or add ice cubes to the hot roasting tin to create a burst of steam, then immediately close the door. This will help develop a good **crust**. Bake for 10 minutes, then reduce the oven temperature to 200°C (180°C fan), 400°F, Gas 6 and bake for another 25–30 minutes or until golden. To **test** if the loaves are done, tap them on the base – they should sound hollow. **Cool** them on a wire rack before slicing or **storing** them. Best eaten within 5 days.

Challah

This traditional Sabbath bread is a challenge, but can be mastered with a little practice. For a neat plait, the dough should be firm but not hard; if too soft the plait loses its definition.

700g strong white bread flour, plus extra for dusting
10g fine sea salt
7g sachet fast-action dried yeast
250ml lukewarm water
100ml sunflower oil or 85g unsalted butter, melted and cooled
3 medium eggs, at room temperature
2 tablespoons soft-set honey

To finish the dough
1 medium egg beaten with a pinch of salt, to glaze
sesame seeds, poppy seeds or sunflower seeds, for sprinkling

HANDS-ON TIME:
40 minutes

HANDS-OFF TIME:
2¼ hours

BAKING TIME:
35–40 minutes

MAKES:
1 large loaf

SPECIAL EQUIPMENT:
large baking sheet

STORAGE:
Once cold, wrap in clingfilm or pop into freezer bags and freeze for up to 1 month

1. Put the bread flour and sea salt into a large mixing bowl or the bowl of a food-mixer and **mix** well with your hand or the dough hook attachment. Sprinkle the dried yeast into the bowl and mix thoroughly. Make a well in the centre.

2. Pour the lukewarm water and sunflower oil or melted unsalted butter into the same measuring jug. Add the eggs and the soft-set honey and beat everything with a fork until the eggs are broken up. Pour the liquid into the well and gradually draw the flour into the liquid using your hand or the dough hook on the slowest speed. It should make a soft but not sticky dough. If there are dry crumbs at the bottom of the bowl or the dough feels stiff or dry, work in more lukewarm water a tablespoon at a time. If the dough sticks to your fingers and clings to the sides of the bowl, work in a little more flour.

3. Dust your fingers and the worktop with flour, then turn out the dough and **knead** it well for 10 minutes or 5 minutes using the dough hook on its slowest speed. The dough should feel firmer and very smooth and pliable, it needs to be stretchy so you can shape it, but firm enough to keep its shape when it's plaited. If you think it feels a little soft, add in a little more flour. Put the dough back in the bowl and cover the bowl tightly with clingfilm or a snap-on lid, or pop it into a large plastic bag and close tightly. Leave to **rise** on the worktop at normal room temperature for about 1½ hours until doubled in size. If your kitchen is hot or it's a sunny day, try to put the dough somewhere a little cooler– if the dough gets too hot or rises too fast it is harder to shape. Line the baking sheet with baking paper.
Continued

Try Something Different

If you're avoiding dairy, use oil in this bread, but if not, use melted butter. To add a bit of texture and a speckled effect, add 2 tbsp poppy seeds to the flour with the salt.

4. Punch down (**knock back**) the risen dough with your knuckles to deflate it, then turn it out onto an unfloured worktop and gently knead it a couple of times. Weigh the dough and divide it into four equal portions. Using your hands, roll each piece on the unfloured worktop to make a 33cm sausage of even thickness. Lay all four ropes on the prepared baking sheet and pinch them together at one end. Turn the baking sheet so that the ropes are lying vertically in front of you, side by side and slightly apart, with the join at the top. Now take the far-left strand under the two middle ones, then back over the last one it went under.

5. Then take the far-right strand and put it under the twisted two in the middle, then back over the last strand it went under.

6. Keep doing this until all the dough strands are plaited.

7. Pinch the ends together and tuck them under the end of the plait neatly.

8. Slip the baking sheet into a large plastic bag, letting in some air so that the plastic doesn't stick to the dough, and close tightly. Leave the plait to **prove** at normal room temperature for 45–50 minutes until almost doubled in size. You want the plait to keep its shape, so don't leave the dough in a warm spot, or for too long, as the dough will over-prove.

9. Towards the end of the rising time, preheat the oven to 230°C (210°C fan), 450°F, Gas 8. Uncover the loaf and carefully brush a thin layer of egg glaze (made up of 1 medium egg beaten with a pinch of salt). Leave it for a minute, then brush with a second fine layer to give it a lovely glossy shine. Sprinkle over the sesame seeds, poppy seeds or sunflower seeds, then bake for 15 minutes. Reduce the oven temperature to 200°C (180°C fan), 400°F, Gas 6 and bake for a further 20–25 minutes until the challah is a rich golden brown. Have a peek at it after 15 minutes and if the plait isn't colouring evenly, turn the sheet. To **test** if the bread is cooked, tap the loaf on the base – it should sound hollow. When fully baked, put on a wire rack to **cool** before storing. Best eaten within 5 days or toasted.

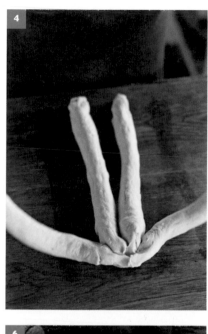

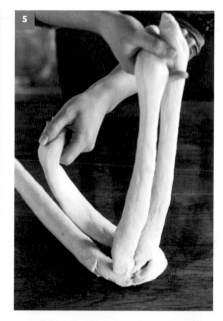

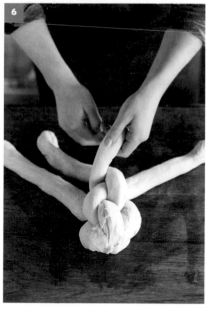

Old-fashioned
English Muffins

The good old English muffin is a challenging bake, but the end result is worth it. They get their characteristic flat tops by being lightly squashed. Ideal for sweet or savoury toppings.

350g strong white bread flour
100g plain white flour, plus extra for dusting
5g fine sea salt
7g sachet fast-action dried yeast
150ml lukewarm water
200ml lukewarm milk
fine cornmeal or polenta, for dusting

HANDS-ON TIME:
40 minutes

HANDS-OFF TIME:
2 hours

BAKING TIME:
22–24 minutes

MAKES:
8 muffins

SPECIAL EQUIPMENT:
2 baking sheets;
Heavy griddle or very heavy-based frying pan

STORAGE:
Once cold, wrap in clingfilm or pop into freezer bags and freeze for up to 1 month

1. Put the bread flour and plain white flour into a large mixing bowl or the bowl of a food-mixer with the sea salt and **mix** well with your hand or the dough hook attachment. Sprinkle the dried yeast into the bowl and mix thoroughly. Make a well in the centre.

2. Pour the lukewarm water and the lukewarm milk into the well and mix with your hand or the dough hook attachment on the slowest speed. It should make a very soft, fairly sticky dough. If there are dry crumbs at the bottom of the bowl or the dough feels stiff or dry, add some more lukewarm water, a tablespoon at a time.

3. Now **knead** the dough in the bowl with your hand for about 10 minutes – this dough is a little different, so the best way to knead it is to slap it against the sides of the bowl – or use the dough hook on the slowest speed for 5 minutes until it feels very elastic, silky-smooth and soft but only slightly sticky.

4. Cover the bowl tightly with clingfilm or a snap-on lid, or pop it into a large plastic bag and close tightly. Leave to **rise** in a warm but not hot spot for about 1 hour until doubled in size.

5. Punch down (**knock back**) the dough to deflate it, then turn out onto a lightly floured worktop and knead for 5 minutes or 3 minutes using the dough hook on the slowest speed. Put the dough back in the bowl, cover as before and leave to rise for 30 minutes. *Continued*

6. Now it's time to shape the dough. Liberally sprinkle fine cornmeal or polenta onto one of baking sheets and flour your hands and the worktop. Turn out the soft dough and divide it into 8 pieces (you can do this by eye or weight it to get 8 evenly sized muffins), then **shape** each piece into a soft, rough ball.

7. Alternatively, and more traditionally, squeeze off a tennis ball-size of dough from the ball through a ring made by joining the thumb and forefinger of one hand and drop the ball straight onto the prepared baking sheet.

8. Once you have a sheet of 8 muffins (they should look slightly scruffy, we're not looking for perfection) spaced well apart so they have room to expand, sprinkle them generously with more fine cornmeal or polenta, and cover them with the second baking sheet. This will give them their traditional flat tops. Leave to **prove** and rise in a warm place, just as they are, for 30 minutes.

9. When you are ready to cook the muffins, heat an ungreased griddle or frying pan until moderately hot. Put the muffins, a few at a time, so as not to crowd the pan, onto the griddle or pan, turning them upside down so that the side that was uppermost is now flat down on the surface of the griddle. Cook the muffins slowly for about 12 minutes, adjusting the heat if you need to so that they are cooked all the way through but not burnt on the outside, then carefully turn them over and cook for a further 10–12 minutes. To see if the muffins are ready, gently press the sides, they should spring back, and the top and bottom should be a good golden colour.

10. As soon as they are cooked remove them from the griddle and wrap in a clean, dry tea towel to keep warm while you cook the rest. Eat warm as soon as possible or leave to cool, then split and toast.

Baguettes

To make iconic 'French sticks' you ideally need high-protein French flour, but a combination of strong flour and the softer, lower protein plain flour works well.

300g strong white bread flour
200g plain white flour, plus extra for dusting
7g sachet fast-action dried yeast
about 300ml lukewarm water
8g fine sea salt
fine cornmeal or polenta, for sprinkling
3g fine sea salt (or ½ teaspoon) dissolved in 4 tablespoons cold water, for brushing

Needs a little skill

HANDS-ON TIME:
1 hour

HANDS-OFF TIME:
6–7 hours or 8 hours overnight + 2 hours

BAKING TIME:
20 minutes

MAKES:
2 baguettes

SPECIAL EQUIPMENT:
Large baking sheet or pizza baking stone; Roasting tin

STORAGE:
Best eaten the same day or the next day

1. **Mix** together the strong white bread flour and plain white flour in a large bowl or the bowl of a food-mixer, then tip half into a separate smaller bowl and put to one side. Stir ½ teaspoon of the dried yeast into the flour in the larger bowl, then work in the lukewarm water, using your hand like a paddle, until you get a smooth, thick batter. Cover the bowl with clingfilm or a snap-on lid, and leave on the worktop for 4–5 hours until the surface is covered with tiny bubbles. (If you use water from the cold tap you can leave the mixture for 8 hours or overnight.)

2. Uncover the bowl and stir 1 tablespoon lukewarm water into the batter. Mix the rest of the yeast and the sea salt into the flours in the second smaller bowl, then gradually work into the batter using your hand or the dough hook attachment on the slowest speed. The dough should be slightly soft but not sticky. If the dough feels very sticky or doesn't hold its shape, add a little more of either flour; if the dough feels tough and dry or there are stray dry crumbs in the bowl, work in more lukewarm water, a tablespoon at a time.

3. Lightly dust your hands and the worktop with flour, then tip the dough out of the bowl. **Knead** it well for about 10 minutes or 5 minutes using the dough hook on the slowest speed, until it feels smooth, very elastic and stretchy.

4. Put the dough back into the bowl, cover it tightly with clingfilm or a snap-on lid, or pop it into a plastic bag and close tightly. Leave to **rise** on the worktop for about 1 hour until doubled in size.

5. Lightly dust your hands and the worktop with flour, then gently turn out the risen dough. Don't punch it down but cut it into 2 equal portions using a sharp floured knife. Without handling the dough too much, shape each piece into a rough ball. Cover loosely with a dry tea towel or clingfilm and leave for 15 minutes.
Continued

6. Move one piece of covered dough to the side for now. Dust the rolling pin with flour, then gently roll each piece of dough into a rectangle about 25 × 30cm. Roll up the rectangle fairly tightly from one long side, like a Swiss roll.

7. Tuck in the ends and pinch the seam firmly. Move the roll of dough to an unfloured part of the worktop and roll it back and forth with your hands to make a 40cm long sausage with gently tapering ends.

8. Lay a large, dry tea towel on a large tray or board and generously dust it with flour. Gently lift the shaped loaf and put it on one side of the floured cloth. Do the same with the second loaf and place it on the tea towel, pleating the cloth in between the loaves to act as a barrier and a support (you could create walls using the rolling pin under the cloth along one side and tins of food, or a thin bottle along the other). Cover everything loosely with clingfilm or a large dry tea towel, and leave to **prove** and rise for about 45 minutes until doubled in size.

9. While the loaves are rising, preheat the oven to 230°C (210°C fan), 450°F, Gas 8. Put the baking sheet or pizza baking stone in the oven to heat up and a roasting tin in the bottom of the oven.

10. When the loaves are ready for baking, quickly remove the hot baking sheet/pizza baking stone from the oven and lightly sprinkle it with fine cornmeal or polenta. Slide and roll the loaves onto it and quickly brush them with the salty water (made up of 3g fine sea salt dissolved in 4 tablespoons cold water). Make several long, deep slashes along the length of the loaves with a small, sharp knife. Put them in the oven and quickly pour a jug of cold water or add ice cubes to the hot roasting tin to create a burst of steam, then immediately close the door. This will help create a good **crust**.

11. Bake the loaves for about 20 minutes or until a really good golden brown and crisp. For an extra crunchy crust, carefully slide the loaves off the baking sheet/pizza baking stone and onto the oven shelf and bake for another couple of minutes. **Cool** on a wire rack and eat the same or next day.

Ciabatta

Making ciabatta is a real test of a baker's skill. It is made in stages, starting with a biga, or 'saved dough' that is slowly fermented to add flavour and liveliness to the soft dough.

For the biga
200g strong white bread flour
50g plain white flour, plus extra for dusting
1 teaspoon caster sugar
1 teaspoon fast-action dried yeast (from a 7g sachet)
200ml lukewarm water

To finish
350ml lukewarm water
3 tablespoons extra virgin olive oil
400g strong white bread flour
100g plain white flour
7g sachet fast-action dried yeast
10g fine sea salt
fine cornmeal or polenta, for dusting

Needs a little skill

HANDS-ON TIME:
40 minutes

HANDS-OFF TIME:
1½–15½ hours or overnight +3½ hours

BAKING TIME:
20 minutes

MAKES:
3 medium loaves

SPECIAL EQUIPMENT:
2 baking sheets;
Dough scraper

STORAGE:
This is best eaten the same day

1. Start by making the biga: put the strong white bread and plain white flour with the caster sugar (this feeds the yeast and keeps it going) into a large mixing bowl. **Mix** well with your hand, stir in the dried yeast, then pour in the lukewarm water and mix it all together to make a fairly sticky dough. Beat the dough with your hand, slapping it against the sides of the bowl for 2 minutes, then cover the bowl tightly with clingfilm. Leave to **rise** at normal room temperature for 8–12 hours (or overnight). The dough will rise enormously and then collapse, but don't be alarmed, this is what it should do!

2. To finish the dough, the next day uncover the biga and pour the lukewarm water and olive oil into the bowl. Work the liquids into the dough with your hand by squeezing the mixture through your fingers and beating with your hand to make a smooth batter.

3. Mix the strong white bread flour with the plain white flour in a separate bowl, then tip half into a third bowl. Add the 7g fast-action dried yeast to the flours in one bowl, and the 10g fine sea salt to the flours in the other bowl.

4. Add the flours with the yeast to the bowl with the biga and mix in with your hand to make a thick, sticky batter-like dough. Beat this dough in the bowl with your hand, slapping it up and down, for 5 minutes until it has stretched and become very elastic. Cover the bowl tightly with clingfilm and leave in a warm spot for about 2 hours until it is 2½ times its original size.

5. Uncover the dough and add the flour/salt mixture, and work it in with your hand to make a soft, sticky dough. Work and **knead** the dough in the bowl for a couple of minutes until you can turn it out onto an unfloured worktop.

Continued

6. Knead the dough well by gathering it up (with the help of a dough scraper) and throwing it down onto the worktop. Do this for 8–10 minutes or until the dough feels silky-smooth and elastic, but also still soft and sticky. Put the dough back in the bowl, cover again and leave to rise in a warm place for about 1 hour until doubled in size.

7. Towards the end of this time, gently warm the baking sheets in a warm oven for 5–10 minutes (you can then turn off the oven), then line with baking paper and dust generously with fine cornmeal or polenta.

8. Using the dough scraper, carefully scrape out the risen dough onto the worktop that has been lightly dusted with flour – don't punch it down or deflate the dough, treat it very delicately.

9. Using a well-floured dough scraper or sharp knife, divide the dough into three roughly equal lengthways strips – they don't need to be neat. Using the scraper, carefully transfer the strips to the warmed lined baking sheets, spacing them well apart.

10. Now use your fingers to gently stretch, not press, the dough into slipper-like shapes – at a very rough size of 30 × 8cm – and try not to disturb all the big bubbles. Don't worry about the uneven, rustic look, the perfect ciabatta is all about the texture and appearance of the crumb.

11. Sprinkle lightly with flour, then slip the sheets into large plastic bags, letting in some air so that the plastic doesn't stick to the dough, and close tightly. Leave to **prove** and rise in a warm place for 30 minutes until almost doubled in size.

12. Towards the end of the rising time, preheat the oven to 230°C (210°C fan), 450°F, Gas 8. Uncover the loaves and bake for about 20 minutes until golden brown. **Cool** on a wire rack and eat warm from the oven, or the same day. The breads can also be split and toasted or grilled.

Brioche
Loaf

The perfect breakfast bread, brioche is rich and buttery, yet light and delicate. The dough is prepared with three risings, which are crucial to create its mouthwateringly soft texture.

375g strong white bread flour, plus extra for dusting
5g fine sea salt
7g sachet fast-action dried yeast
4 medium eggs, chilled
about 4 tablespoons milk, chilled
175g unsalted butter, diced
1 egg beaten with a pinch of salt, to glaze

1. Put the bread flour into a large mixing bowl or the bowl of a food-mixer. Add the sea salt and **mix** in with your hand or the dough hook attachment. Stir in the dried yeast and make a well in the centre.

2. Break the eggs into a measuring jug, break them up with a fork – but don't froth them up – then add enough chilled milk to make up the liquid to 250ml. Pour this into the well, then gradually work in the flour using your hand or the dough hook on the slowest speed. It should make a soft and very sticky dough. If there are dry crumbs at the bottom of the bowl or the dough feels stiff or dry, work in a little more milk, a tablespoon at a time.

3. Using the dough scraper, turn out the dough onto a lightly floured worktop and **knead** it well for 10 minutes or 6 minutes using the dough hook on its slowest speed. The dough will feel slightly firmer and more elastic. Gradually work in the butter, a few pieces at a time until the dough feels silky smooth, soft and still a bit sticky. When you've mixed in all the butter and you can't see any streaks, scrape the dough back into the bowl and cover the bowl tightly with clingfilm or a snap-on lid, or pop it into a large plastic bag and close tightly. *Continued*

Up for a challenge

HANDS-ON TIME:
30 minutes

HANDS-OFF TIME:
4–4½ hours

BAKING TIME:
40–45 minutes

MAKES:
1 medium loaf

SPECIAL EQUIPMENT:
450g loaf tin (about 19 × 12.5 × 7.5cm); Dough scraper

STORAGE:
Once cold, wrap in clingfilm or pop into freezer bags and freeze for up to 1 month

4. Put the bowl in the fridge to **rise** for 2 hours until the dough doubles in size.

5. Flour your knuckles and punch down (**knock back**) the dough to deflate it. Reshape it into a ball, then cover it tightly once more with clingfilm and return it to the fridge for 1 hour. Meanwhile, grease the tin with butter and line the base and two long sides with a long strip of baking paper.

6. Turn out the dough onto a floured worktop and knead it gently for 1 minute. Cover it loosely with clingfilm and leave to rest for 5 minutes. Lightly flour your fingers and gently pat out the dough into a rectangle 16 × 25cm. Using a sharp knife, cut the rectangle into three thick strips lengthways, leaving the strips attached at one short end.

7. Plait the strips until you reach the end of each piece.

8. Tuck the ends under to seal the plait.

9. Lift the dough into the prepared tin. Don't pat or prod the dough plait to get it to fill the tin, it will naturally do that as it proves. Slip the tin into a large plastic bag, letting in some air so that the plastic doesn't stick to the dough, and close tightly. Leave it to **prove** and rise in a warm but not hot place (you don't want all that lovely butter to melt) for 1–1½ hours until doubled in size.

10. Towards the end of the rising time, preheat the oven to 220°C (200°C fan), 425°F, Gas 7. Uncover the risen brioche and lightly brush it all over with 1 egg beaten with a pinch of salt, but be careful not to 'glue' the dough to the tin. Bake for 15 minutes, then reduce the oven temperature to 180°C (160°C fan), 350°F, Gas 4 and bake for a further 25–30 minutes until well risen and a deep golden brown. To **test** if the bread is done, tap the base of the loaf – it should sound hollow; if there's a dull 'thud', carefully return the loaf to the tin and bake it for a further 5 minutes and test again. Leave until completely **cool** on a wire rack before slicing – handle gently – then **store**. Best eaten within 4 days or toasted.

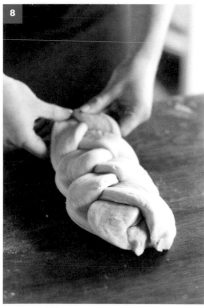

Harvest
Wreath

This rich loaf makes a showstopper centrepiece, perfect for eating with cheeses, cold meats and soups. It's made from two doughs – one that's plaited, and one for the decorations.

For the dough

about 650g strong white bread flour, plus extra for dusting
7g sachet fast-action dried yeast
300ml lukewarm milk
2 medium eggs, at room temperature
10g fine sea salt
1 tablespoon linseeds
2 teaspoons cumin seeds
100g raisins
100g soft-dried cranberries
100g pecans, roughly chopped
100g unsalted butter, at room temperature, cut into small flakes

For the decoration

250g strong white bread flour
½ teaspoon fine sea salt
¼ teaspoon fast-action dried yeast (from a 7g sachet)
about 165ml water, at room temperature
1 egg beaten with a pinch of salt, to glaze

HANDS-ON TIME:
1½ hours

HANDS-OFF TIME:
2½–3 hours
+ 30 minutes

BAKING TIME:
30–35 minutes

MAKES:
1 large loaf

SPECIAL EQUIPMENT:
Large baking sheet;
Leaf-shaped cutter
(optional)

STORAGE:
Once cold, wrap in clingfilm or pop into freezer bags and freeze for up to 1 month

1. To make the dough, put 400g of the bread flour into a large mixing bowl and **mix** in the dried yeast with your hand. Make a well in the centre.

2. Add the eggs to the lukewarm milk in a jug and beat with a fork to combine. Pour the liquid into the well and stir it into the flour mixture with your hand to make a smooth, thick, batter-like dough. Cover the bowl with clingfilm and leave in a warm spot for 20 minutes until it is bubbly and has expanded a little.

3. In a separate bowl, combine the sea salt, linseeds, cumin seeds, raisins, soft-dried cranberries and roughly chopped pecans with half of the remaining flour (125g). Break up any clumps of fruit.
Continued

6. Knead for another 2 minutes, then rest for 5 minutes as before. Knead again for 2 minutes, then put the dough back in the bowl and cover tightly with clingfilm. Leave to **rise** in a warm but not hot place for 1½–2 hours until doubled in size.

7. Punch down (**knock back**) the dough to deflate it, then cover the bowl with clingfilm and leave to rise for about 1 hour until doubled in size.

8. While the dough is rising, make the dough for the decoration. Mix the 250g strong white bread flour and the ½ teaspoon fine sea salt in a separate mixing bowl, then stir in the ¼ teaspoon fast-action dried yeast. Make a well in the centre and pour in about 165ml room-temperature water and mix everything together with your hand to make a fairly firm dough. Turn out onto a lightly floured worktop and knead for 10 minutes. Cover the bowl tightly with clingfilm and refrigerate until needed. Line the baking sheet with baking paper.

4. Uncover the batter and stir in all the fruits and nuts, mixing everything together with your hand. Add the 100g flaked unsalted butter and squeeze the mixture together with your fingers for about 5 minutes until it makes a very heavy, sticky dough. Cover the bowl again and leave in a warm place for 10 minutes.

5. Sprinkle some of the remaining 125g flour onto the worktop and scrape the dough out onto it. Flour your hands and **knead** the dough gently for 2 minutes, working in enough of the remaining flour to make a soft dough that doesn't stick to your hands. Cover the dough on the worktop with the upturned bowl and leave to rest for 5 minutes.

9. Punch down the risen fruit and nut dough and turn out onto a lightly floured worktop. Knead gently for a few seconds to make a neat ball, then weigh the dough and divide it into three equal portions.

10. Using your hands, roll each portion on the worktop to make a neat and even sausage about 70cm long. Join the three strands together at one end and plait them together, as neatly and tightly as you can.

11. Join the ends of the plait together to make a wreath about 25cm across.

12. Very carefully lift the wreath onto the prepared baking sheet and tweak it if it's lost any of its shape. Cover loosely with clingfilm and leave on the worktop to **prove** while you preheat the oven and make the decorations.

Continued

13. Preheat the oven to 180°C (160°C fan), 350°F, Gas 4. Roll out the chilled dough on a floured worktop to about 4mm thick and, using a sharp knife or a leaf-shaped cutter, cut out 5 leaves. If you happen to have a small vine leaf about 7cm across, you could cut around it or trace the shape onto thin card to use as a template. If you're feeling confident and artistic, you could cut the leaves freehand. Using a small sharp knife, score the leaves with veins.

14. Use the rest of the dough to make grapes the size of hazelnuts and small peas. You will need 9–12 grapes for each bunch, but there's plenty of dough, so make your own designs, adding tendrils or more trailing vines.

15. Uncover the wreath and lightly brush it with 1 egg beaten with a pinch of salt, then stick on the vine leaves and grapes in triangular bunches, using the egg glaze as glue if you need to. Leave the wreath uncovered on the worktop until it has almost doubled in size – if the kitchen is warm this might just take a couple of minutes, but don't let it over-prove or the shapes will be lost and all your hard work will be in vain.

16. Carefully brush the wreath all over with the glaze. Bake for 30–35 minutes until a good golden brown. If the top starts to become too dark during baking, cover with a sheet of foil and rotate the baking sheet if necessary so that the loaf colours evenly.

17. Leave the loaf to **cool** and firm up on the baking sheet for 5 minutes, then slide the wreath on its paper onto a wire rack. Leave until completely cold before slicing and getting ready to **store**. Best eaten within 5 days.

Sourdough from Scratch

Bread from a sourdough starter has a deep flavour, wonderful crust and chewy crumb. This loaf is a challenge, but once mastered add wheat or rye flakes, seeds, nuts, olives or dried fruit.

1.5kg organic strong white bread flour
10g fine sea salt

Making the sourdough starter

Day 1

Put 100g of the white bread flour into a small bowl. Boil 115ml filtered tap water and let it cool until just lukewarm, then pour it into the flour and mix it with your fingers to make a thick sticky paste. Cover the bowl with a dampened tea towel or piece of muslin secured with an elastic band, but don't seal the bowl with clingfilm or a lid otherwise it won't capture and grow the natural or 'wild' yeasts (fungi) that are in the air. Leave it in a draught-free spot on the kitchen worktop, re-dampening the tea towel as necessary. You can give it a boost by putting the bowl near a bowl of fruit. The yeasts will begin to grow and produce tiny bubbles (carbon dioxide) and lactic acid, which will eventually leaven and flavour the dough. Make a note of the date so you can keep track.

Day 2

Dampen the tea towel or muslin.

Day 3

Dampen the tea towel or muslin.

Day 4

Remove the tea towel or muslin and examine the paste – it should have a skin and look bubbly. Now smell it – it should have a milky tang, but if it smells offensive rather than slightly sour, or if you spot mould, or there are no signs of activity, then sadly you'll have to chuck it away and start again. If your starter looks healthy, it's time for the first feed! Add another 115ml cooled boiled water to the bowl, mix in with your fingers, then work in another 100g of the flour to make a thick, gooey paste. Work the mixture vigorously with your hand for 1 minute to incorporate plenty of air, which will encourage the yeasts to grow. The mixture should now be double its original quantity so if you need to transfer it to a larger bowl so it can continue to expand. Cover the bowl as before and leave for 24 hours on the worktop.
Continued

HANDS-ON TIME:
1½ hours

HANDS-OFF TIME:
7 days + 8–16 hours

BAKING TIME:
35–40 minutes

MAKES:
1 medium loaf

**SPECIAL
EQUIPMENT:**
Baking sheet or pizza baking
stone; 20cm cane
banneton (optional);
Roasting tin

STORAGE:
Once cold, wrap
in clingfilm or pop
into freezer bags and
freeze for up to
1 month

Day 5

There should be a lot of action going on in the starter now, so stir it well with your hand or a plastic spatula, then remove and discard half of the mixture. Work in another 115ml cooled boiled water, then 100g of the flour, mixing well with your hand. Cover the bowl as before and leave overnight (or for at least 12 hours) on the worktop.

Day 6

The starter should be very active now, with plenty of bubbles; if it seems a bit sluggish but it's definitely still alive, repeat the procedure for Day 5. If it looks in good shape, it's time for another feed. You need to nurture the starter so it has enough energy to make a loaf and increase the volume so you'll have enough for your first loaf and some left over for the next one. Work in 100ml cooled boiled water, then 100g of the flour to make a soft, sticky batter. Cover as before and leave overnight.

Day 7

The dough mixture should be very bubbly by now, so scrape it into a larger bowl and work in 250ml cooled boiled water and 200g of the flour. Cover and leave overnight again.

Day 8

At last, it's baking day!

Add 350ml cooled boiled water and 300g of the flour to the starter, mix well, then cover and leave on the worktop for 4–6 hours so the batter-like dough is thick and bubbly. Measure out enough starter to make the loaf and scoop the rest into a clean plastic tub (an old ice-cream container is perfect) with a couple of holes punctured in the lid. Store in the warmest part of the fridge and feed it regularly, every 5 days or so – discard (or give away) half of it, then work in enough flour and water to get it back to its original quantity. Don't worry if you have to leave it for a week or so while you're on holiday, just remember to give it some TLC when you return. When you want to make the next loaf, bring the starter back to room temperature, then feed it, as for Day 8, stirring well, and leave for about 4 hours until bubbly. If your starter has become very sour-smelling and makes your eyes water, stale or slow to become active, then halve and feed it every 8 hours until it is restored to health and is bubbly with a pleasant milky aroma. Don't worry if your starter separates into a clear liquid on top of the thick paste – if it is pale, stir it in, but if it is darkish, pour it off, stir the starter well and feed as normal.

To make the loaf

700ml lively starter
about 400g of the flour
10g fine sea salt

1. Scrape 700ml lively starter into a large mixing bowl or the bowl of a food-mixer. Add about 100g of the flour and the sea salt and work in using your hand or the dough hook attachment on the slowest speed. Once this has been fully mixed in, gradually work enough flour to make a soft but not sticky dough – how much you need depends on the consistency of the starter and the flour you are using.

2. Turn out the dough onto a lightly floured worktop and **knead** it well for 10 minutes or 5 minutes using the dough hook on the slowest speed until smooth and elastic. Put the dough back *Continued*

in the bowl then cover the bowl tightly with clingfilm or a snap-on lid, or pop it into a large plastic bag and close tightly. It is really important to leave it to **rise** in a warm place now until doubled in size. This can take from 2–6 hours, depending on the vigour of the starter as well as the temperature of the dough. These doughs are a bit more forgiving than regular yeasted doughs, though, and they will cope with a bit of neglect if you're running late.

3. Turn out the risen dough and gently **shape** it into a neat ball – if the dough is too soft to hold its shape, add in a little more flour. If using a banneton, set the ball, rounded-side down, into the well-floured basket, then slip the banneton into a large plastic bag and close tightly. If not, set the ball, rounded-side up, onto a sheet of lightly floured baking paper and cover with a large upturned bowl.

4. Leave to **prove** in the warm kitchen (if it's chilly, turn on the oven early to add a bit of warmth) for 2–4 hours until doubled in size.

5. Towards the end of the rising time, preheat the oven to 230°C (210°C fan), 450°F, Gas 8 and put the baking sheet or pizza baking stone into the oven to heat up, along with a roasting tin in the bottom of the oven.

6. When the loaf is ready, uncover it and remove the heated baking sheet or pizza baking stone from the oven. If the loaf has been proved in the banneton, set a sheet of baking paper on the baking sheet, or dust it with flour, and quickly invert the loaf onto it and load it into the oven. If you have proved the dough on the baking paper, quickly lift it, on the paper, onto the hot sheet or stone and load it into the oven. Quickly pour a jug of cold water or add ice cubes to the hot roasting tin to create a burst of steam, then immediately close the door. This will help create a good **crust**. Bake for 35–40 minutes until the loaf turns a good golden brown. To test if the bread is done, tap it on the base – it should sound hollow. Transfer to a wire rack and leave to **cool**, then **store**. Eat within 6 days or toast it.

Nine-strand Plaited Loaf

This elaborate loaf is not for the faint-hearted. It is made from three layers of dough – a four-strand saffron plait, a three-strand black olive plait and a twisted fresh herb dough.

Up for a challenge

For the saffron dough
½ teaspoon saffron strands
150ml hand-hot water
500g strong white bread flour
25g unsalted butter, at room temperature, diced
8g fine sea salt
7g sachet fast-action dried yeast
1 teaspoon soft-set honey
1 medium egg, at room temperature, beaten
about 125ml milk, at room temperature

For the black olive dough
75g stoned black olives, finely chopped

For the Herbes de Provence dough
500g strong white bread flour
25g unsalted butter, at room temperature, diced
2 teaspoons finely chopped fresh Herbes de Provence (a mix of oregano, basil, thyme and rosemary)
8g fine sea salt
7g sachet fast-action dried yeast
1 medium egg, at room temperature, beaten
about 275ml water, at room temperature

To finish
1 medium egg beaten with a pinch of salt, to glaze

HANDS-ON TIME:
2 hours

HANDS-OFF TIME:
2¼ hours + 1–6 hours to soak the saffron

BAKING TIME:
40–45 minutes

MAKES:
1 large loaf

SPECIAL EQUIPMENT:
Large baking sheet; 6 long bamboo skewers

STORAGE:
Once cold, wrap in clingfilm or pop into freezer bags and freeze for up to 1 month

1. Start by making the saffron dough. Crumble the saffron strands into a small heatproof dish, pour over the hand-hot water and leave to soak for at least 1 hour or up to 6 hours – the longer the better. For a really deep flavour, preheat the oven to 180°C (160°C fan), 350°F, Gas 4 and toast the crumbled saffron in the heatproof dish for 8–10 minutes, until slightly darker, then add the water.

2. When you're ready to make the saffron dough, put the white bread flour into a large bowl or the bowl of a food-mixer. Rub in the butter with your fingertips until it disappears. Stir in the sea salt, then the dried yeast, and make a well in the centre.

3. Pour the saffron liquid into the well and add the soft-set honey, beaten egg and 100ml of the room-temperature milk. Gradually work the flour into the liquids in the well, using your hand or the dough hook attachment on the slowest speed. Add more milk as you need it to get a dough that feels slightly firm rather than slightly soft. The texture is important – a stiff, dry dough or one that is too firm will be as hard to plait as one that's slightly sticky or very soft.
Continued

4. Turn the dough out onto a lightly floured worktop and **knead** it well for 10 minutes or 5 minutes with the dough hook on the slowest speed until it is very stretchy, pliable and the dough keeps its shape — you may have to knead in a little flour. Put the dough back in the bowl, then cover the bowl tightly with clingfilm or a snap-on lid and leave to **rise** at room temperature for about 1½ hours until doubled in size.

5. While this dough is rising, make the Herbes de Provence dough. Put the 500g strong white bread flour into a large mixing bowl and rub in the 25g unsalted butter with your fingertips. Add the 2 teaspoons finely chopped fresh Herbes de Provence and the 8g fine sea salt and mix in thoroughly with your hand or the dough hook attachment. Sprinkle the 7g fast-action dried yeast into the bowl and mix in. Make a well in the centre, then pour in the medium beaten egg and 250ml of the room-temperature water and gradually work the flour into the liquids in the well, using your hand or the dough hook on the slowest speed. Add more water if you need it to make a slightly firm dough (as in Step 3). Turn out the dough and knead it well (as in Step 4). Weigh the dough, cut off two-fifths and put it into a separate bowl. Cover the bowl tightly with clingfilm and leave to rise at normal room temperature for about 1 hour until doubled in size.

6. Add the 75g stoned and chopped black olives to the larger ball of dough and gently knead in on a lightly floured worktop until evenly distributed — if the dough feels very sticky and soft, knead in a little extra flour. Put this dough back into the bowl in which the dough was made, cover the bowl tightly with clingfilm and leave to rise alongside the two other doughs for about 1 hour until doubled in size. Line the baking sheet with baking paper.

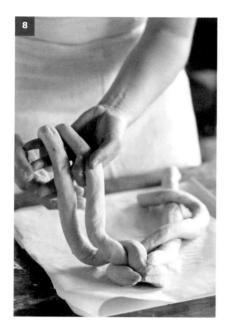

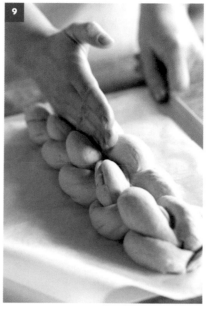

7. Punch down (**knock back**) the risen saffron dough to deflate it, then turn it out. Weigh the dough and divide it into 4 equal portions. To make the four-strand plait, roll each portion of dough with your hands to make an even rope 35cm long. Set the ropes on the prepared baking sheet and pinch them together at one end. (They may be longer than the sheet, but don't worry.) Arrange the ropes vertically in front of you, side by side and slightly apart with the join at the top. Now, run the far-left strand under the 2 middle ones, then back over the last one it went under.

8. Then run the far-right strand under the twisted 2 in the middle, then back over the last strand it went under. Keep doing this until all the dough is plaited. Pinch the ends together at the bottom of the plait and tuck them under to make a neat shape.

9. Punch down (knock back) the risen black olive dough to deflate it and turn it out. Weigh the dough and divide it into 3 equal portions. To make the three-strand plait, roll each portion of dough with your hands to make a rope 40cm long. Set the ropes side by side and slightly apart on the worktop. Pinch them together at one end, then plait them together in the usual way. With the edge of your hand, make a deep indentation lengthways along the
Continued

centre of the four-strand plait, then set the three-strand plait on top of the four-strand one on the baking sheet and tuck the ends under the bottom plait.

10. Punch down (knock back) the remaining Herbes de Provence dough to deflate it and turn it out. To make the two-strand twist, roll the dough with your hands to make a thin rope 75cm long. With the index finger of your left hand (if you are right-handed; use your right hand if you are left-handed) press down on the middle point of the rope, then wind the two strands together around your finger to make a neat twist.

11. With the edge of your hand, make a deep indentation along the length of the three-strand plait, as before, then set the twist on top, and tuck the ends under the loaf.

12. To make sure the loaf keeps its shape as it proves and doesn't topple to one side, insert 6 bamboo skewers vertically into the dough: set one skewer in the dough 5cm from each end, then 4 equally spaced between them. Brush very lightly with egg glaze, then leave to **prove**, uncovered, at cool room temperature, for 35–45 minutes until almost doubled in size – it's important that the plait keeps its shape, so don't leave it in a warm spot or over-prove the dough. Towards the end of the rising time, preheat the oven to 230°C (210°C fan), 450°F, Gas 8.

13. Carefully brush the loaf with a thin layer of 1 medium egg beaten with a pinch of salt to glaze. Leave it for a minute, then brush with another fine layer, which will give you a glossier bread. Bake the plait for 10 minutes, then reduce the oven temperature to 190°C (170°C fan), 375°F, Gas 5 and bake for 30–35 minutes until the plait is a rich golden brown and smells deeply aromatic. To test the bread is done, tap it on the base – it should sound hollow. Carefully transfer to a wire rack and leave to **cool** before gently removing the skewers. Best eaten with 5 days or toasted.

Herby Brioche Croissant Rolls

An extravagant combination of France's two favourite breakfast breads, these rolls are rich, buttery and delicate with a sponge-cake crumb beneath a light, flaky crust.

HANDS-ON TIME:
1¾ hours

HANDS-OFF TIME:
4½–4¾ hours

BAKING TIME:
40–50 minutes

MAKES:
10 rolls

SPECIAL EQUIPMENT:
24cm springclip tin; Pizza wheel-cutter (optional)

STORAGE:
Once cold, wrap in clingfilm or pop into freezer bags and freeze for up to 1 month

For the dough

375g strong white bread flour, plus extra for dusting
5g fine sea salt
10g caster sugar
7g sachet fast-action dried yeast
5 tablespoons milk, chilled
4 medium eggs, chilled and beaten
175g unsalted butter, at room temperature, diced

For the filling

100g unsalted butter, cool and firm but not hard
1 rounded tablespoon finely chopped mixed herbs (such as parsley, thyme, oregano and rosemary)
2 garlic cloves, or to taste, finely crushed
1 medium egg beaten with a pinch of salt, to glaze

1. Start by making the dough. Put the bread flour, sea salt and caster sugar into a large mixing bowl or the bowl of a food-mixer and thoroughly combine with your hand or the dough hook attachment. **Mix** in the dried yeast.

2. Add the chilled milk and the eggs to the bowl and work in with your hand or the dough hook on slowest speed to make a very soft and sticky dough. Dust your hands and the worktop with flour and **knead** the turned-out dough really well for 10 minutes or 6 minutes with the dough hook on a slow speed. Gradually work in the butter, a few pieces at a time, to make a silky-smooth, soft but still sticky dough. When the dough starts to look evenly coloured and you can't see any streaks of butter, scrape it back into the mixing bowl and cover the bowl tightly with clingfilm or a snap-on lid, or pop it into a large plastic bag and close tightly.

3. Put the dough in the fridge to **rise** for 2 hours until doubled in size, then flour your knuckles and punch down (**knock back**) the dough to deflate it. Cover it again and put it back in the fridge for 1 hour.

4. While the dough is chilling, make the garlic butter filling. Mash the unsalted butter with the mixed herbs and crushed garlic cloves until it is easy to spread but not oily.
Continued

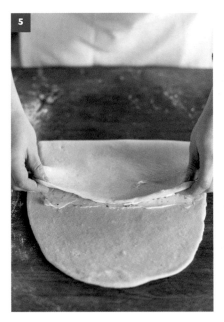

5. Lightly flour the worktop, then turn out the dough and roll it out with a lightly floured rolling pin into a rectangle 18 × 54cm. With one short edge in front of you, spread the butter evenly over the lower two-thirds of the rectangle. Fold the top third of the rectangle over the middle section, then fold over the third from the other side to make a three-layer 'sandwich'. Press the open edges with the side of your hand to seal.

6. Give the dough a quarter turn so that the rounded folded edge is to the left, a bit like the spine of a book, and the part-open edge is on your right. Roll out the dough to a rectangle as before and fold it in three again. Seal the edges and give the dough a quarter turn, then roll and fold one more time.

7. Wrap the dough in clingfilm and chill for 45–60 minutes until the dough is cool and firm. Grease the tin with butter and line the base with baking paper.

8. Roll out the dough on a lightly floured worktop to a rectangle 30 × 30cm. Trim and neaten the edges with a pizza wheel-cutter or a large, sharp knife, then roll up the dough like a Swiss roll from one short edge and pinch the seam to seal. Flour a large, sharp knife and cut the roll into 10 equal pieces. Set the rolls cut-side up and slightly apart in the prepared tin. Brush very lightly with the 1 medium egg beaten with a pinch of salt to glaze, but don't 'glue' the dough to the sides of the tin.

9. Slip the tin into a large plastic bag, letting some air in so that the plastic doesn't stick to the dough, and close tightly. Leave to **prove** and rise in a warm but not hot place, otherwise the butter will ooze out, for about 45 minutes until almost doubled in size.

10. Towards the end of the proving time, preheat the oven to 220°C (200°C fan), 425°F, Gas 7.

11. Uncover the risen rolls and brush them with the egg glaze, then bake for 25–30 minutes until they are a good chestnut brown and have a rich, 'toasty' aroma. Set the tin on a heatproof surface and carefully unclip the sides, leaving the crown of rolls on the metal base, then return it to the oven for 5 minutes to crisp up the sides. **Cool** slightly on a wire rack before serving and pulling apart. Best eaten warm the same day.

What bread shall I bake?

Conversion Table

WEIGHT		VOLUME		LINEAR	
Metric	**Imperial**	**Metric**	**Imperial**	**Metric**	**Imperial**
25g	1oz	30ml	1fl oz	2.5cm	1in
50g	2oz	50ml	2fl oz	3cm	1¼in
75g	2½oz	75ml	3fl oz	4cm	1½in
85g	3oz	125ml	4fl oz	5cm	2in
100g	4oz	150ml	¼ pint	5.5cm	2¼in
125g	4½oz	175ml	6fl oz	6cm	2½in
140g	5oz	200ml	7fl oz	7cm	2¾in
175g	6oz	225ml	8fl oz	7.5cm	3in
200g	7oz	300ml	½ pint	8cm	3¼in
225g	8oz	350ml	12fl oz	9cm	3½in
250g	9oz	400ml	14fl oz	9.5cm	3¾in
280g	10oz	450ml	¾ pint	10cm	4in
300g	11oz	500ml	18fl oz	11cm	4¼in
350g	12oz	600ml	1 pint	12cm	4½in
375g	13oz	725ml	1¼ pints	13cm	5in
400g	14oz	1 litre	1¾ pints	14cm	5½in
425g	15oz			15cm	6in
450g	1lb	**SPOON MEASURES**		16cm	6½in
500g	1lb 2oz	**Metric**	**Imperial**	17cm	6½in
550g	1lb 4oz	5ml	1 teaspoon	18cm	7in
600g	1lb 5oz	10ml	2 teaspoons	19cm	7½in
650g	1lb 7oz	15ml	1 tablespoon	20cm	8in
700g	1lb 9oz	30ml	2 tablespoons	22cm	8½in
750g	1lb 10oz	45ml	3 tablespoons	23cm	9in
800g	1lb 12oz	60ml	4 tablespoons	24cm	9½in
850g	1lb 14oz	75ml	5 tablespoons	25cm	10in
900g	2lb				
950g	2lb 2oz				
1kg	2lb 4oz				

Index

Acknowledgements

Hodder & Stoughton and Love Productions would like to thank the following people for their contribution to this book:

Linda Collister, Laura Herring, Caroline McArthur, Sam Binnie, Helena Caldon, Alasdair Oliver, Kate Brunt, Laura Del Vescovo, Joanna Seaton, Sarah Christie, Anna Heath, Damian Horner, Auriol Bishop, Anna Beattie, Rupert Frisby, Jane Treasure, Sharon Powers.

The author would also like to thank Alan Hertz, Barbara Levy and Simon Silverwood.

First published in Great Britain in 2015
by Hodder & Stoughton
An Hachette UK company

1

Copyright © Love Productions Limited 2015
Photography Copyright © David Munns 2015

The right of Linda Collister to be identified as the Author of the Work has been asserted by her in accordance with the Copyright, Designs and Patents Act 1988.

BBC and the BBC logo are trademarks of the British Broadcasting Corporation and are used under licence. BBC logo © BBC 1996.

A CIP catalogue record for this title is available from the British Library

Hardback ISBN 978 1 473 61532 8
Ebook ISBN 978 1 473 61531 1

Editorial Director: Nicky Ross
Editor: Sarah Hammond
Project Editor: Laura Herring
Series Editor: Linda Collister
Art Director: James Edgar
Layouts: Nicky Barneby
Photographer: David Munns
Food Stylist: Natalie Thomson, Lizzie Harris
Props Stylist: Victoria Allen

Typeset in Dear Joe, Mostra, Kings Caslon and Gill Sans
Printed and bound in Italy by L.E.G.O. Spa

Hodder & Stoughton policy is to use papers that are natural, renewable and recyclable products and made from wood grown in sustainable forests. The logging and manufacturing processes are expected to conform to the environmental regulations of the country of origin.

Hodder & Stoughton Ltd
Carmelite House
50 Victoria Embankment
London EC4Y 0DZ

www.hodder.co.uk

Continue on your journey to star baker with the other titles in *The Great British Bake Off: Bake It Better* series, the 'go to' baking books which give you all the recipes and baking know-how you'll ever need.

DON'T JUST BAKE. BAKE IT BETTER.